Other People's Money clears up the mystery of how to find the money for your business. Harold Lacy's proven techniques can successfully guide business owners towards their business funding. My office HIGHLY recommends the book to our clients.

JAYNE REITER, DIRECTOR,
SMALL BUSINESS DEVELOPMENT CENTER

The material is a '10.'

AUDIO PUBLISHERS ASSOCIATION

Harold Lacy is like hiring a money 'detective.' He knows where to find the money for any business venture. He has effectively combined his 25 years experience as a successful banker and entrepreneur to share the most up-to-date information on creative financing methods. Read this book twice. It is that good!

RON SCHAEFFER, CPA

Other People's Money provides the entrepreneur with a 'machete' to cut a path through the money 'jungle.' Using proven insight, Lacy explains just about everything you need to know about 'angels,' bankers, non-traditional sources, and more important, how to get them to COMMIT! This is a valuable book for people seeking business financing.

BOB MOOK, SMALL BUSINESS STRATEGIES
EDITOR, *DENVER BUSINESS JOURNAL*

Financial authority Harold Lacy straightforwardly explains the pros and cons of financial backing from commercial banks to venture capitalists. Lacy's no-nonsense style and advice makes this a valuable resource for entrepreneurs seeking sources and strategies for funding all types of businesses.

BOOKLIST

Harold Lacy is the 'Money Doctor' for business. *Other People's Money* provides rare insight into the motivations and needs of investors. More importantly, the book provides the critical information on how to get the money people to commit.

ROBERT STAREKOW, PRESIDENT,
SILVERHEELS RESTAURANT

If you are dead serious about starting or expanding a business, it's unlikely you'll get more complete financing information anywhere else.

THE MEEKER HERALD

Harold Lacy has a unique insight that brings 'order' to the 'chaos' of pursuing funding for a new product. *Other People's Money* is the Bible of business financing.

Your extensive financial information was one of the highlights of the 1997 International Franchise Expo in Washington, D.C. We had over 25,000 attendees for the Expo. Your financial seminar received the highest marks.

HOORAY for this insightful and all-inclusive guide to obtain business financing! Harold's advice and tips over the past 20 years have helped me to expand my operations from one ReMax office to nine offices, plus a mortgage company, title company, insurance company and a real estate development company. If it worked for me, it can work for you!

Other People's Money provides valuable insight into the important matching needs of the entrepreneur with that of the investors/bankers. Harold has been on both sides of the financing 'table' as a successful banker and entrepreneur.

Other People's Money provides something else few other business books do - - it gives you sources for those small amounts of start-up money which rarely comes from banks. Anyone who is tired of being told what they can't do and why they can't finance their dreams should read this book.

Not only does *Other People's Money* identify the locations of business funding, but provides a detailed road map of HOW to get the money. It has replaced several MBA courses and hours of frustration in looking for money. A MUST read for a new or emerging business.

FINANCING YOUR BUSINESS DREAMS
WITH

OTHER PEOPLE'S MONEY

The supreme accomplishment is to blur the lines between work and play.

ARNOLD TOYNBEE

FINANCING YOUR BUSINESS DREAMS
WITH

OTHER PEOPLE'S MONEY

How and Where to Find Money for Start-up and Growing Businesses

HAROLD R. LACY

Sage Creek Press

Traverse City, Michigan

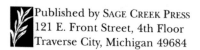
Published by SAGE CREEK PRESS
121 E. Front Street, 4th Floor
Traverse City, Michigan 49684

Publisher's Cataloging-in-Publication Data
Lacy, Harold, R.
    How to finance your business dreams with other people's money: how and where to find money for start-up and growing businesses / Harold R. Lacy - - Traverse City, MI: Sage Creek Press, 1998.
       p. cm.
    Includes bibliographical references and index.
    ISBN 1-890394-11-4
    1. Small business—finance. 2. I. Title.
HG4027.7 .L33   1998   97-76470
658.15'92   dc—21 CIP

PROJECT COORDINATION BY JENKINS GROUP, INC.

02 01 00 99 ◆ 5 4 3 2

Printed in the United States of America

To my wonderful daughters, Kirsten and Kimberly.
To my loving wife, Nancy, whose encouragement and
support made another dream come true.

CONTENTS

PREFACE

*It is better to entertain an idea than to take it home to
live with you the rest of your life.*

DAMON RUNYON

STAYING OPEN TO CHANGE

L ET'S LOOK AT A VERY SUCCESSFUL COMPANY THAT TEMPORARILY
pulled in its business antenna and put the company on auto-
matic pilot. That company? IBM.

IBM was so proud of its sales record and huge profits made on
mainframe computers for the corporate market that management
ignored the growing demand for the personal computer. They
ignored the rapid technological changes that were driving down
prices while dramatically improving the performance level of personal computers.

While the market research department had pulled in its business
antenna, start-up companies building personal computers were
showing potential investors studies that indicated the growing market for personal computers and that brand loyalty would soon be secondary to price and performance.

These true entrepreneurs possessed the important outlook that
the proverbial glass of water is half full. They ignored those who
ridiculed them by saying, "You're going into competition with IBM,
which controls over 70 percent of the computer market? No way!"

These people just did not get the big picture. They focused on the

11

established market for computers rather than on the much larger market for tools that make our lives easier and save us time.

Change is all around us and will always be with us. We can never go back to the "good old days," if they ever really existed. The only thing different about change today is its increasing speed.

You've probably had the experience of walking on a treadmill at your local health club or YMCA. As you increased the speed of the treadmill, you found that you had to walk faster to keep up. Change is like the increasing speed of the treadmill, but more like the one used to test the capabilities of your heart. Now the doctor is in control of the speed, not you, and he is gradually increasing the speed.

That's the way change works in the world today. That "invisible hand" keeps turning up the speed so that changes are happening faster and faster. To keep from falling off the back of the treadmill of change, we are forced to rely on timesaving devices such as cellular phones, fax machines, answering machines, pagers, and microwave ovens, just to keep up with the faster pace.

TAKING CONTROL

Your imagination is your preview of life's
coming attractions.

ALBERT EINSTEIN

But we can take control of our lives. We can buy ourselves a job — with other people's money — if we are willing to commit ourselves to the task.

I would like to share with you a thought about commitment by W. H. Murray, a leader of the Scottish Himalayan Expedition. (This, by the way, was shared with me by a true inspirational mentor of mine, Paul Karasic, founder of the American Seminar Leaders Association.)

ON BEING COMMITTED

Until one is committed, there is a hesitancy, a tendency to draw back always, ineffectiveness concerning all acts of initiative and creativeness. There is one elementary truth the ignorance of which kills countless ideas and splendid plans: at the moment that one definitely commits, then Providence moves, too. All sorts of things occur to help one that would never have occurred. A whole stream of events stream from that decision, raising in one's favor all manner of unforeseen incidents, meetings and material assistance which no person could have dreamt would come their way.

I have also learned a deep respect for one of Goethe's couplets: "Whatever you can do or dream, begin it. / Boldness has power, magic, and genius in it."

Use this book to help you begin to realize your dreams. It is divided into six chapters. Within each chapter, there is a discussion of the mechanics of using other people's money for your own goals, plus an extensive list of helpful resources.

Remember, this book was written from the viewpoint and shared experience of a person who has been there many times. Enjoy what you're about to learn and prosper.

A smooth sea never made a skilled mariner.
ENGLISH PROVERB

INTRODUCTION

Persistence will give you power to prevail
over all problems.

I RECOMMEND THAT ONE SHOULD READ CHAPTERS 1-6 IN ORDER. THIS will give you an overall view of the many financial sources available. This is very important since most entrepreneurs make the mistake of focusing on only ONE source for their financing.

After you have completed chapters 1-6, I recommend the following plan of "action" to get started on pursuing your financing sources:

Chapter 6	Business Plan
Chapter 3	Banks and Bankers
Chapter 1	Formal and Informal Investors
Chapter 2	SBA Programs
Chapter 4	Non-Bank Alternatives
Chapter 5	Buying a Business—Financing Sources

You may be asking, "Why weren't the chapters arranged to follow the 'action plan'?" I have learned from my seminars that most people are aware of the importance of the business plan. What they are REALLY interested in learning are WHERE to find money and HOW to approach and deal with the different money sources. Eighty-five percent of start-up businesses are funded by "angels." That is why "angels" are discussed in Chapter 1.

You may also be asking, "Then why is the chapter on banks and bankers listed before "angels," which is discussed in the chapter on formal and informal investors?" There are several important reasons for meeting with the bankers prior to meeting with "angel" and other sources of financing.

1. It is a tremendous learning process to find out the criteria that the financing/investor world is looking for in a company. The money world is "uncharted territory" for most people seeking funding for their business.

2. The banker will provide a "free" critique of your business plan and its feasibility.

3. The feedback and criticism from the banker should be used to "polish" your business plan to overcome objections from other lenders/investors.

4. The banker will lay out the issues that prevent the bank from committing to your request. Issues such as inadequate cash flow, weak managerial experience, inadequate secondary financial support, etc. Now that you have been "turned down," go back and review the banker's criticism(s). Assess the criticisms to see if they can be overcome. For example, offering of a "limited" guarantor to overcome the lack of secondary financial support; obtain additional written commitments from potential customers that will allow you to revise your cash flow statement to meet the banker's requirements.

5. Even if you are not able to obtain some of your initial financing from the banker, you will have obtained an invaluable lesson in dealing with other money sources such as "angels." You usually only have one chance with an "angel," so you want to make the very best presentation possible.

6. Last, but not least, the banker can be a tremendous resource for directing you to a financing source that meets your needs. The banker has a tremendous network of alternative lenders and investors. Don't be afraid to ask the banker for referrals to his sources that would be a good match for your type of funding request.

Secret: The fastest and most efficient method of obtaining funding is to utilize the "piggyback" approach. "Piggyback" financing utilizes a **combination** of financing sources together to obtain the total amount of funding needed for the business.

An example of "Piggyback" financing is when you need $50,000. It is much easier to combine several financing sources that will be discussed in Chapters 1-6. For example:

"Angel" investor	$15,000
Bank loan	15,000
Lease financing	10,000
Accounts Receivable financing	5,000
Your funds	5,000
TOTAL	$50,000

Using this "Piggyback" financing is very successful since there is a feeling among lenders/investors that if someone else is in the "deal," there is a greater comfort level.

You might be asking yourself, "Wouldn't it be a lot easier and save time just to have one financing source for the entire $50,000?" Yes, it would. The challenge is that there are fewer people who have $50,000 available for investing as compared to the vast number of people who have $5,000-$20,000 available. Most investors like the comfort level of knowing that there are other investors sharing the risk.

In this book, we will be sharing with you the full spectrum of financing sources available to new and growing businesses. We will explore such areas as organizing your needs, planning your approach, and writing your business plan. We'll investigate formal and informal venture capital, delve into government funding, outline how to develop a winning relationship with your banker, explain leasing and reveal alternative funding strategies.

We hope to achieve three objectives:

- ◆ Identify the various sources of financing available to you.

- ◆ Learn the advantages and disadvantages of each type of financing source.

- ◆ Help match your financing needs with the right financing source.

WHY YOU NEED THIS BOOK NOW

In the past few years, there have been many changes in the business world and job markets. These changes are driving a record number of people out of the roller-coaster corporate world and into something that they have some control over: being their own boss by owning their own business. This can mean buying a business or franchise, or starting a business from scratch.

As recently as seven to ten years ago, most people thought of a job as something you stepped into once you graduated from high school or college and stayed with for a long time. Many people would remain with the same company for their entire working lives, then get the gold watch and the nice retirement plan. Anyone who started or purchased a business was not envied. Why? With your own business, you had no job security. You worked lots of extra hours for no prestige and no company benefits.

My, how quickly times have changed. The cover story in the February 26, 1996, issue of *Newsweek* was titled "Corporate Killers." It featured pictures of CEOs of a dozen major corporations such as AT&T, IBM, Scott Paper, Delta Airlines, Chemical Bank, Boeing, Sears Roebuck, General Motors and others. Below each picture appeared the number of jobs the CEO had eliminated during the previous 12 months. IBM: 60,000 jobs. AT&T: 40,000. Boeing: 28,000. Sears: 50,000. General Motors: 74,000. And on, and on, and on, for a total of 374,000 jobs at 12 companies in just one year.

These companies are not fly-by-night operations; they have been an integral component of our economy and way of life for years. This is not a temporary situation of downsizing, rightsizing, corporate layoffs, cast-offs, whatever you call them. It is a profound shift in the way our economy works.

A recent report by the Department of Labor indicated that people in the 35-50 age group can expect three to five *career* changes by the time they reach retirement. That's three to five career changes, not job changes. This is going to be pretty traumatic for most people, having the boss say to them, "We don't need you anymore, Fred, not because of the job you've been doing, but because we have to improve our bottom line. We have to improve our return to the stockholders." Wall Street loves layoffs!

BUYING YOURSELF A JOB

But many people — you might be one of them — have had just about enough of constantly being in fear losing their jobs because of a corporate decision. There is a new term for those who are opting to get out of the rat race. We say they are "buying themselves a job."

When people buy a business or franchise or start a new business, they are really buying themselves a job. And whenever you buy something, you have to pay for it somehow. With any large-ticket item — a car, a house, a boat — financing is the key. Very few of us are able to write that check right out of our checkbook.

It is the same for buying a business. Financing is the key to opening the door to that American dream of being your own boss. What is financing after all but using other people's money to achieve your goals? The challenge of financing is not that there aren't enough funds available. The challenge today is finding the right source of funding that meets the needs of you, the borrower, in terms of the interest rate, terms of repayment, collateral, guarantee of the spouse, the application process and the turnaround time it takes to obtain these funds.

How It Works

Let me share with you my personal experience with using other people's money to finance one of my dreams. In 1991 I was contacted by two members of a local athletic club that had been taken over by a bank when the developer defaulted on another real estate project. Although the club had been successful in the past, the bank had to close it when the developer came in during the middle of the night and removed all of the athletic equipment, weights, desk, inventory, telephones; you name it, it was gone.

After six months of bureaucratic procrastination, the bank finally decided it would bite the bullet and reopen the club, which meant spending close to $450,000 dollars in the purchase of new equipment and working capital to get the business going again. The only smart thing the bank did is hire an experienced manager to start rebuilding the club and its membership.

When I was contacted by the two members, we reviewed the current situation of the club:

1. The new manager had been able to rebuild the membership from zero to 1100 members in less than a year; the club would reach the break-even point within two to four months.

2. The bank was under tremendous pressure from the board of directors and examiners to get rid of the loan: sell the club and get the loan off the books.

Just to test the waters, we made a ridiculously low offer of $225,000. To our great surprise, the bank accepted it.

Then came the fun part of putting together a loan package. We finally came up with a bank loan of $125,000 secured with equipment and accounts receivable, and a $100,000 investor loan for a 5 percent share of the club. This combination of bank loan and investor financing allowed us to finance 100 percent of the purchase price with not one dime of our own money.

That was 1991. Today the membership of the Lakewood Athletic Club has grown from 1100 members to over 2500. The original bank loan was paid off in 18 months with the increased cash flow from new memberships. The club is doing extremely well, is rated in the top clubs in the nation, and I'm in the process of selling out to my partners for a sizable profit. Of course $1 would have been a profit when you remember that we had none of our own money invested.

> *While someone is busy telling me it cannot be done, others are busy doing it.*
>
> HENRY FOSDICK

REMEMBER THE BASICS

Why would anyone want to sell when the business is doing so well? Just remember four basic words of investing: Buy low, sell high.

Sounds simple, but it's much harder to put into practice. Just talk to a few stock market investors who waited just a little too long to get out and took a big hit. Timing is the key; don't be greedy. There is plenty of money available out there, if you can communicate effectively to the right source of lending.

Communicating effectively means having a winning business plan, one that communicates in the language of lenders — both traditional and nontraditional — and investors. They are looking for written documentation of what you and your product or service are all about, something they can read and analyze.

But before you are ready to sit down and write your business plan, it is critical to determine your attitude toward commitment and change. Do you possess the necessary traits found in successful entrepreneurs who look upon change as opportunity? Whenever there is change, there are winners and losers. The losers are the ones who did not have their business antennas up, picking up how the needs of the market were changing.

Show me someone who has done something worthwhile,
and I'll show you someone who has overcome adversity.
                                                    LOU HOLTZ

1

FUNDING SOURCES: FORMAL AND INFORMAL

There is only one success—to be able to spend your life in your own way.

CHRISTOPHER MORLEY

OVERVIEW

IN THIS FIRST CHAPTER, WE WILL DISCUSS FORMAL AND INFORMAL VENture capital investors — there is a major difference. We will talk about the things you should look for in the ideal investors, and itemize the do's and don'ts of approaching them. We will outline the five-step process for interviewing and screening prospective investors and, finally, we will share the top six reasons why funding requests are rejected by investors and lenders.

INTERNAL AND EXTERNAL SOURCES

When looking for capital, first decide whether it should come from internal or external sources.

1. Internal sources are your own assets and liquidity. Self-financing is composed of actual cash investments or equities held in real estate or partnerships. These can be used as capital in the business or used as collateral on a loan to inject capital into the business. By utilizing self-financing, you maintain total control over the business.

2. External sources can be banks, suppliers, finance companies, leasing companies, etc.

It is important to understand that in most cases of external financing, lenders are looking for some amount of internal financing that has already been put in place. They are looking for the owner's commitment or "blood equity" backed up with some dollar amount.

Even if you can't generate all the capital requirements internally, it will be very attractive to an outside investor to demonstrate that you have enough confidence in the business that you've been able, through your resources, to generate some of the capital needed. It is very rare, indeed, to see an outside investor fund 100 percent of a business when the owner has not demonstrated his or her ability or creative ingenuity to come up with a share of the capital.

An excellent way of combining the internal with external funding sources is to inject your own funds into the business and use the guarantee of the co-signer for the balance. For example, after completing a cash flow forecast (this is covered in more detail in Chapter 6 on business plans), it is determined that you need $50,000 and that you have only $20,000 in liquid assets and equities to inject into the company. It is much easier to obtain outside investors who will co-sign or guarantee a loan for $30,000 once they have seen that you've already injected your own funds into the business.

ANGELS AND VENTURE CAPITALISTS

Let's compare informal and formal funding sources.

1. **Venture Capitalists.** This is probably one of the most misunderstood and overused terms in today's list of financing sources for small businesses. You may even have heard someone say to a budding business person who has been turned down for a loan, "Go talk to a venture capitalist. They finance high-risk companies."

   The actual number of start-up businesses funded through venture capital sources in 1995 was 270. That is less than .001 of 1 percent of the businesses launched that year. You can see why we're not going to spend much time on formal venture capitalists as a source of funding for most small businesses.

2. **Angels.** The more viable source for funding for the start-up or existing business is the informal venture capitalist, or angel, because **angels provide more than 85 percent of the funding for start-up businesses**.

   The term originated during the 1800s in New York City, in the early days of Broadway. Since the production of Broadway plays was — and still is — a high-risk venture, banks would not even listen to loan proposals from producers. But the show must go on, so the producers approached a group of prominent, successful businessmen for the financing. Because of the glamour of being associated with the theater, this group took the risk and provided the capital on very fair terms without stringent requirements and equity control. For their magnanimity, the investors were called angels.

   The term now refers to any outside investor who provides the initial capital for new or risky business, is very fair about repayment and other loan requirements and does not take advantage of the business owner's situation.

   Angels are a key source of funding for the business that does not have a track record and is seeking that initial funding. And they are all around us.

IDENTIFYING ANGELS

First, let's prepare a list of potential angels you may already know: Your doctor, or any doctor you are acquainted with. Your dentist, lawyers, accountants, financial planners, insurance agents, fellow entrepreneurs, business owners, associates of yours in professional and social organizations, relatives, friends, former employers, former employees, potential suppliers, customer clients and financial consultants.

You may be thinking, "I bought this book for the inside information that I should contact my rich brother-in-law for funding my business? How do I get my money back?" Just hold that thought.

What you have done is assume that this list of contacts is the ultimate list of angels. Wrong. They are just the bridge to a much bigger pool of potential investors and lenders. You must look upon these contacts as the springboard to their network of contacts. That's where you will find your angels.

Review your list to make sure that the people on it have the critical common denominator: They associate or work with clients or friends that have excess capital to invest. For example, your insurance agent. She might not necessarily have the excess capital to invest herself, but she works with and associates with hundreds of clients and friends who probably fit your investor profile.

> *If you win a man to your cause, you will first have to convince him that you are his sincere friend.*
> ABRAHAM LINCOLN

Now do the same for your doctor, attorney, friends, relatives, and so on. You can see the potential network pool of investors gets very

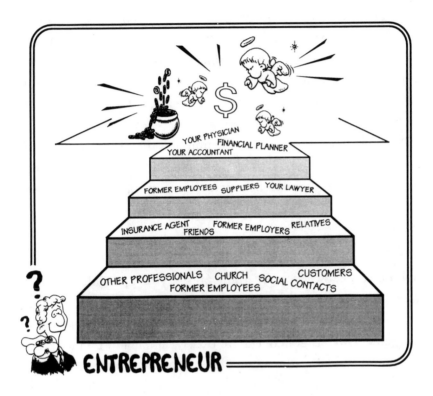

large very quickly. Again, think of these contacts as the bridge to other people they know who have access to money and are looking for some type of investment. If you focus just on the initial list, you are short-changing yourself over 99 percent of the potential networking contacts that these people have developed over the years.

A recent study showed that the average person is surrounded by about 250 friends and relatives. Now take your list. Let's just say you have 6 people listed as potential contacts. By multiplying each one of these possible contacts by 250, you could come up with 1,500 potential sources for the funding of your business.

Secret: Think of your many contacts as a means to an end—money for your business.

You can also add to your potential angel pool by looking through your local newspaper. There's generally a section in the business or classified ad section called "Business Opportunities" or "Capital Available." These ads usually say something like: I have $20,000 to invest in an on-going business, or, I have $15,000 to invest in a start-up, early stage development company.

With nothing to lose except the time you spend with that person, you can't afford not to follow up. Otherwise, you'll never know if that could have been the perfect match for you, if that could have been your angel.

UNDERSTANDING ANGELS

How do you know if you are in the presence of a possible angel? He most likely has been in the business arena for a number of years, has been successful and has recently sold the business or taken early retirement. Angels generally have excess capital and financial security, but are missing the substance that motivated them for all of those years: the drive of playing the business game, of dealing with the daily challenges of business and developing solutions to these challenges.

At this stage of life, they're not too anxious to re-enter that arena of daily battles, but they are looking for a chance to use their experience and expertise in a growing company that will allow them to reestablish their identity and contacts. When they're meeting with their buddies at the golf club or at a social occasion, the first question that always seems to come up is, "What are you doing now that you sold your business or retired?" The typical response of "Well, playing lots of golf, or traveling" will quickly end most conversations.

But if they can say that they've just become an investor in a small growing company that provides supplies and equipment to the snow-board industry, which, as we know, is growing very rapidly, it gets other people's attention. The angel gets the satisfaction of being able to share with their friends and associates new information and that makes the angel feel good about himself, gives him something to look forward to and provides an identity at the same time.

Another common trait of angels is that often they have become bored with their own careers or jobs and are looking for something that will provide excitement to their lives. The excitement of sharing new and different experiences, like being an investor in a small growing company, appeals to those driven by the excitement of risk/reward situations.

When you help others to grow, you grow yourself.

There's even the somewhat benevolent notion of an older angel assisting a young entrepreneur.

*The best exercise on earth is to reach down and pull a
person up.*

In Robert J. Gaston's book, *Finding Private Venture Capital for Your Firm,* he provides the profile of a typical informal investor or angel.

- ◆ Occupation: Close to 70 percent of all angels are business owners or managers.

- ◆ Age: Angels are generally 20 years older than the entrepreneurs they are financing.

- ◆ Gender and Race: Close to 84 percent of all angels are white males.

- ◆ Education: Over 70 percent have a college degree.

- ◆ Income: The average annual income for an angel is $90,000.

- ◆ Wealth: The average net worth of an angel is $750,000.

- ◆ Deal Acceptance Rate: 20 percent. This rate is not bad when you compare it to less than .001 percent for formal venture capital firms.

◆ Co-Investors: Only 1 of 12 angels is a sole investor.

FIVE CHARACTERISTICS OF THE IDEAL INVESTOR

There are five characteristics that you should look for in the ideal investor. Your investor or investors might have only a few of these traits. That's fine, but the more traits that they have, the greater benefit to you. It will be the icing on the cake made out of money.

1. **Experience.** Experience not necessarily limited to the area of your particular business, but successful experience with business or businesses, preferably with a new growing company or one that has successfully overcome previous business challenges.

2. **Understanding of the risks involved in the business.** You want someone who is emotionally stable to deal with the sometimes roller-coaster growth cycles of a business.

3. **Ability to inject additional funds into the business** if the business starts growing faster than expected. Additional capital is a necessity and a paradox when a business starts growing rapidly. Most people think that more and faster growth will solve cash flow problems, but actually it creates a greater demand for capital. So having an investor who can provide or have access to additional funds for this growth is important.

4. **Mutual agreement on when and what type of exit will take place for the company.** In other words, how and when is the investor going to be repaid? Is it going to be through a long-term payment program that will start within the next couple of years? Or will it come from the sale of the business? Or will it

be from refinancing from other sources such as the bank? This needs to be discussed and agreed upon prior to obtaining and investing the funds in the business. Once the money is invested, it is very difficult, and sometimes impossible, to come to agreement as to how the investor is going to get the money back and when.

5. **Emergency backup.** You should have available to you not only the investor's advice and counsel when needed, but also meaningful assistance if an emergency comes up, such as rapid growth or illness.

THE INDIRECT APPROACH: THE KEY TO FINDING THE MONEY

> **Secret:** The Indirect Approach....this is the technique that is utilized by professional fund-raisers and money people—IT WORKS!!

Now that you know what angels look like and where to find them, how do you use your contact list to reach them? For starters, here's what not to do:

Have you ever had a good friend or relative verbally share his or her idea of how he or she is going to make you rich, if you just part with a little bit of your money, like maybe $25,000? They really hate coming to you for the money, but all their liquidity is temporarily tied up in that new surround-sound TV with the mini-dish, the boat, the snowmobiles, the new RV. Sound familiar?

How interested would the people on your contact list or potential angels be in investing in your business if you approached them that way? We have all been victims of the direct approach. It is not much fun and doesn't get results.

Secret: It is important that you have a clear under-standing of how the "indirect approach" works and can be utilized in your search for funding. Reread this section, if necessary. It is that important.

The key to success when approaching your winning contact list is to use the "indirect approach." When you contact the people on your list do not solicit them for the money. What you want to say is that you respect them for their success and position in the business community and they are the type of person you are looking for as an investor in your company. But — and this is critical — you need to say that you do not want to infringe on your relationship by approaching them to invest in your business. However, you would be very appreciative if they would pass your business plan on to some of their friends or associates who might be in a position and have the interest to invest in a growing company.

You need to tell them that the investment money is not as impor-tant to you as putting together the right team, one that works togeth-er and is on the same page as far as objectives and management goals.

Because you are acting in a professional, businesslike manner, one of two things will happen when you approach your contacts this way.

1. They will start reading the business plan as soon as you leave. You have created a great amount of curiosity about your busi-ness.

    Within a couple of days they will contact you and say, "I have just a few questions I'd like to go over about your business plan." They have contacted you because you have not placed any pressure on them by asking them for their money. You have used the indirect approach, which gets winning results. Your contact has now become your angel.

2. If your contact is not in a position to invest in the business, they will direct your business plan to one or several of their many contacts who will become your ultimate angel.

So you can see, you win either way.

THE LAST ONE IN

> **Secret:** The "Last One In" technique removes any mistrust in dealing with financial matters.

Another effective strategy when meeting with angels is the "last-one-in" approach.

Remember when you were a kid and went swimming with your friends at a new lake? You looked around, no one's in the water. How deep is the water? How cold is it? Are there any creatures in there? Any hidden rocks, tree limbs, or broken glass?

You knew your friends were probably asking themselves the very same questions. But it seems like there's always someone who jumps in first and hollers to the rest of us, "Hey, the water's fine, come on in." Then you see the magic of "the herd" go into action and everybody jumps in.

Most people don't want to be the "first in the water" or in unfamiliar situations such as investing in a new business venture. There is comfort and security knowing that other people are going to be investing in the deal. You can use this bit of human nature to your advantage by telling potential investors that their commitment is contingent upon you raising the balance of the investment from other sources.

Say, for example, that you're trying to raise $25,000. You ask your angel if, once you have obtained commitments for the other $20,000, he would come in at that point with $5,000? Most people will make that commitment, once they see that their participation is contingent upon you raising the balance from other sources. Now go out and contact some more angels and use the same approach. Get the commitment from everyone before they actually have to put the money into the business.

TALKING TO ANGELS

Secret: One of the most often asked questions I hear at my seminars is, "Where do I find these financial 'Angels'?" Attempts to develop a formal "Angel" directory has had very limited success. The reason? "Angels" are usually interested in becoming involved in ONE company at a time. They are usually private people and don't want to see their names on a nationally-distributed "list."

There is a 5-step checklist to follow when interviewing investors. It covers the essential points upon which any business relationship between the two of you will be built.

1. **Have a partnership agreement that is mutually agreed upon.**
   This is vital to spell out the duties and responsibilities of each investor. You need to make sure that it is crystal clear that they have access to the books and information about the business, but they will not be allowed to participate in the day-to-day operations of the business unless you request it. You are the person in control, the captain of the ship. This needs to be spelled out very carefully and agreed upon.

2. **Be positive.** The angel is going to read your reactions and confidence about the business. This will be a very important aspect in the decision-making process, and confidence needs

to be tempered and sincere. It is important to be upbeat and positive in discussing the potential for the business and where you think it's going, but the so-called "cheerleader" type of confidence is often detrimental.

3. **Deal with the investor directly**, not through intermediaries or brokers or on the telephone. You need to be face-to-face with the investor or lender. There are a lot of unscrupulous individuals out there trying to get information about different opportunities. You don't want to be in a position of talking to a possible future competitor, so have a potential investor or lender sign a one-page confidentiality agreement before discussions progress very far.

4. **Listen to the potential investor.** Be open to suggestions. You don't necessarily have to follow any or all of these suggestions, but at least be open to listen, and to take suggestions and ideas under advisement. You can learn the most enlightening things about business is from other entrepreneurs or investors.

5. **Look beyond the cash.** In addition to funds, quite a number of investors have strong financial statements and strong banking ties. They can use their signature as a way of obtaining funds for your business. Sometimes the bank will even use the collateral or equity of the investor as a way of making a loan to the company. This would be a substitute for the cash injection, and definitely a subject to explore.

The biggest step you can take is the one you take when you meet the other person halfway.

WHY "DEALS" ARE REJECTED BY MONEY PEOPLE

> **Secret:** Learning from other people's mistakes leads to success faster.

You'll notice that all our approaches to investors include delivering a written business plan, one that describes how the money is going to be used, the cash flow projections, the background and descriptions of any unique skills of management, the strength and weakness of the competition, and a detailed marketing plan. These are just a few of the key items that investors need to know before investing in any type of business.

We'll talk more about this when we discuss the elements of the winning business plan in Chapter 6, but keep in mind even informal investors need a formal proposal to evaluate before they hand over any money.

The importance of a well-prepared business plan can't be overstated. Just look at what investors say are the most frequent reasons they reject deals:

1. **The business plan was not written from the perspective of the investor or lender.** It did not list the benefits and answer some of the questions and concerns that affect the investor or lender. Often the business plan is written entirely from the perspective of the borrower and doesn't identify the true needs and benefits to the person providing the risk capital. This is covered in more detail in Chapter 6.

2. **Inadequate growth potential.** If the business plan shows a limited future, or a growth potential of less than 25 percent over the next five years, investors will not feel that the return is adequate for their risk capital.

3. **Investors' lack of knowledge of the industry and management**

personnel of the company. The information presented in the business plan does not answer all their questions or leaves them feeling less than confident.

4. **Management's lack of experience or talent in the position of handling the responsibilities of running the business on a day-to-day basis.** The entrepreneur may be good at marketing, but can he or she manage money, hire the "right" personnel, retain the good employees?

5. **Lack of "blood equity" in the business.** The investor has to see proof that the business owner has invested time, energy and funds to get the business to this stage. The investor is looking for the personal investment and commitment of the owner of the business, so there is a sharing of the risk in case the business runs into stormy economic conditions.

6. **The lack of a proprietary interest**, that is, a patent, copyright, or exclusive territory. How difficult would it be for potential competition to enter the marketplace?

Alternative Sources

Another method of alternative financing for start-up businesses is utilizing your credit cards. Although plastic is not a recommended primary source for most businesses, you would be surprised how many businesses have been started through lines of credit on cards.

The key thing to consider, if this is the last option, is to make sure that your profit margins are great enough to cover the 18 percent interest that is usually charged on credit card balances.

It makes a lot of sense to start asking six months to a year ahead of time for an increase in your existing credit card limits in order to get the maximum amounts available. You can take advantage of the new credit card solicitations that we receive almost on a daily basis. A person could obtain, over a year, five credit cards with a limit of $5,000 each, thus creating a $25,000 capital injection, which should be able to fund the majority of start-up businesses.

To give you an idea of the full potential of credit cards as a source of funding for your business, there was an article in the *Rocky Mountain News*, July 22, 1996. During a six-month period, a newspaper reporter collected the credit card company solicitations she had received, for a total of more than $295,000 in credit. Although many of these offers were for credit limits of $1000 to $3000, there were some as high as $10,000, and in one case, the offer extended a line of credit for $28,000.

This should be looked upon as only a short-term financing source which will eventually be replaced by bank financing, investor financing or other sources that will have a lower interest rate. But, at that point, you'll be classified as an existing business.

One of the best kept secrets for locating capital is by placing a well-written ad in the *Wall Street Journal* (1-800-568-7625). There have been large sums of money raised through sources looking at investing in small companies. *Investor Magazine* is also a good source for investors in private companies. The magazine has regional issues for every area of the United States, so that your article can reach investors that are in your area.

Investor Magazine's phone number is 1-800-748-6951. Call if you have an item of interest that might qualify your company for an article.

2

FUNDING SOURCES: GOVERNMENT

A little encouragement can spark a great endeavor.

OVERVIEW

IN THIS CHAPTER WE WILL EXPLORE THE SMALL BUSINESS ADMINISTRATION or SBA. We will discuss SCORE and Small Business Development Centers, both are funded by the federal government and provided as a **free** service to small businesses. We will also look how states, counties and cities have stepped up their funding of small businesses with exciting and creative new programs.

DON'T OVERLOOK LOCAL GOVERNMENT FINANCIAL ASSISTANCE

State and local governments are increasingly eager to help small businesses for two reasons:

1. Cities have been duped in their efforts to attract the glamour names of the Fortune 500 companies. These companies have become skilled in playing one city against another to obtain

generous concessions in the form of property tax and income tax abatements, low-cost industrial revenue bonds to build their plants, and so on. In fact, most of the corporations that took advantage of these financial incentives in the past decade are also at the top of the list of companies downsizing and laying off employees in this country. Thus, the promised job growth hasn't materialized.

2. Numbers from the Department of Labor show very clearly that the new growth in jobs is in small businesses. Local governments are realizing they can get a better return on dollars invested in programs designed to assist small businesses.

One of the major misconceptions about government sources of financing, whether it be from the federal, state or local level, is that these agencies are in the same category as welfare or food stamps. Many small business owners look upon government loan programs as entitlement programs with no stipulations on the types of qualifying businesses, collateral, or repayment. The truth of the matter is that these agencies, although they are operated by the government, now use lending techniques and analyses similar to commercial banks.

Some of these programs are discussed in more detail at the end of this chapter; see the Resource Guide at the back of this book for more information.

THE SBA

Secret: Forget the old "horror stories" about dealing with the SBA. The SBA has become "user friendly" over the past 5 years. Don't overlook some of the new programs that are being developed to provide better financial assistance to the small business.

The Small Business Administration, or SBA, operates a number of programs to identify specific needs that commercial banks have not adequately fulfilled. It is important to understand that the SBA does not make direct loans as an agency. Rather, it assists businesses by making loan guarantees through participating banks and other institutions.

A bank would use the guarantee of the SBA when a loan request does not meet all the bank's requirements for collateral, cash flow, management ability, and the risk of the industry. The bank would like to make the loan but there is a discomfort level with the borrower not meeting all of the bank's credit requirements.

SBA-guaranteed loans do not utilize government funds, but use the money that is on deposit at banks and other institutions. The guarantee is made by the SBA for up to 90 percent of the face value of the loan.

Although the focus of the SBA loan program is to emphasize the repayment ability of a company, the agency still looks at collateral and personal guarantees as a way of "shoring up" a loan request.

SBA PROGRAMS

Some of the more popular SBA loan programs are:

- ◆ The 7A Guaranteed Loan Program

- ◆ The LODOC Loan Program

- ◆ The 504 Debenture Loan Program

- ◆ Micro-Loan Program

- ◆ 8A Program

- ◆ Greenline Program

- ◆ Small Business Investment Corporation

◆ Small Business Development Companies

◆ Economic Opportunity Loans

1. **The 7A Guaranteed Loan Program.** These are loans made for working capital, equipment, acquisitions, purchase and/or remodeling of property, and inventory. The maximum loan amount is $500,000, which the SBA will guarantee up to 75 percent. Some of the collateral that the SBA will consider includes:

   a. publicly traded stocks and bonds

   b. certificates of deposit

   c. savings accounts

   d. cash value of life insurance policies

   e. real estate

   f. accounts receivable

   g. machinery

   h. land and buildings.

The major advantages of a 7A loan are the relatively low down payment requirements and the longer term for repayment, seven to ten years rather than two to five years for banks. In addition to lower interest rates and higher advance rates, the loan can be paid off at any time without a prepayment penalty. This is very important to a business that will need further refinancing down the road due to rapid growth.

2. **LODOC Program.** This is an acronym for LOw DOCumentation. This program, adopted by the SBA in 1992, simplifies the application process to about 3 days, thus reducing the time

---

Secret: This is H O T!!!

and bureaucracy that has been associated with traditional SBA loans. For loan requests under $50,000 there is only a single-page application. For loans of $50,000 to $100,000, the applicant needs to furnish income tax returns for the past 3 years and a personal financial statement, in addition to the single-page application. The LODOC program is the most successful program in SBA's history; loan volume tripled in just the last two years.

3. **504 Debenture Loan Program.** Although this is not primarily for start-up businesses, it is for those businesses that are growing and want to acquire commercial property or equipment. This program was initiated through the help of certified development companies, which fund 40 percent of the loan through a Second Mortgage Debenture. The remaining balance — 60 percent of the loan — is made up of a first mortgage on the property, provided by the participating bank. The borrower only has to provide 10 percent of the bank's down payment portion. Loan terms run between 10 and 20 years, and the rate is fixed. As with the 7A program, the 504 program takes into consideration the number of jobs to be created with the new funds and how it will help the community.

4. **Micro-Loan Program.** The purpose of this program, which was started in 1993, is to provide start-up capital in relatively small amounts of $25,000 or less to those small businesses considered too small by the commercial banks. Proceeds of the loan can be used for working capital, equipment purchases, or as a revolving line of credit. The loan is guaranteed by the SBA and operated by nonprofit organizations that work with small busi-

nesses in securing alternative funding. It is currently operating in 46 states; the average loan size is approximately $10,000 to $12,000. Over half of these loan funds have gone to women-owned businesses with another 30 percent going to minority-owned businesses.

To find out more about the Micro-Loan Program in your area, contact the regional SBA office to obtain the name of the participating nonprofit organization.

5. **8A Program**. This provides specialized management and technical assistance to minorities starting or expanding their businesses. It also provides assistance with government procurement opportunities.

6. **Greenline Program.** This program has been started on a test basis in several states to assist small businesses with working capital lines of credit. The loan is administered through commercial lenders and the loan amounts are based upon the business's level of accounts receivable and inventory, which is usually controlled by an outside resource.

7. **Small Business Investment Corporation.** This type of vendor operates in conjunction with the federal government and provides loans to business start-ups. Every dollar that is invested in the business by the SBIC is matched with $3 to $4 of SBA-guaranteed loans. The advantage to the small business owner is the amount of leverage that is available to a company utilizing the SBIC.

8. **Small Business Development Companies**. The main difference between this financing source and the Small Business Investment Corporation is that the funds come exclusively from private corporations and private businesses. The main focus of the SBDC is for long-term financing as opposed to

short-term working capital. In addition, SBDCs provide counseling and assistance in various aspects of running a small business: technical assistance, training, finance, human resources,
marketing and manufacturing.

See the Resource Guide at the back of this book for names of
Small Business Investment Corporations and Small Business
Development Companies in your area.

9. **Economic Opportunity Loans**. These are funds that are made
available to small businesses owned by persons with low
incomes. To be eligible, the business must be owned at least 50
percent by someone classified as low income who has been
denied financing from banks and other financial institutions
because of economic or social challenges. Repayment on
these loans is very flexible and very generous in providing a
long-term payout, with most loans having to be repaid within
10 years and real estate loans in 25 years.

MORE SBA HELP

In addition to these programs, the SBA also operates the Women's
Loan Program, the Vietnam Veterans Loan Program, the
Handicapped Assistance Loan Program and other minority assistance. Moreover, the SBA has made special provisions to help small
businesses that have been negatively affected by federal pollution
regulations and occupational and safety health requirements.

Another special program offers guarantees for loans to small general contractors to finance the construction or renovation of resi-
dential and/or commercial buildings for ultimate sale. Loans may be
used for the acquisition of properties, immediate construction, sig-
nificant rehabilitation, and the acquisition of vacant land.

The applicant must show a satisfactory ability in constructing and renovating projects and have less than $750,000 outstanding on any SBA loan. Loans are guaranteed up to 90 percent for loans up to $155,000, 85 percent when the loans go up to $750,000. Maturities cannot exceed 36 months, plus a reasonable time for construction or renovation. Principal payment is required in a single payment at the time of sale, with interest payments required semiannually; interest must be paid by the applicant's own resources and not from the loan.

Businesses should contact their local SBA office to receive additional information on these special programs.

SBA LENDERS: THERE IS A DIFFERENCE

> **Secret:** Not all SBA lenders are created equal. Pay close attention to the subtle, but major, difference between preferred and certified SBA lenders. It could make the difference between success and failure in obtaining your funding.

It is important to be aware that all SBA lenders are not the same. The three major categories are:

1. preferred lenders

2. certified lenders

3. participant lenders.

Preferred lenders are both bank and non-bank institutions that have a reliable history of making good credit judgment on loans. Working with preferred lenders reduces the processing time since they can make the final decision on a loan approval without going to the SBA. This is important.

Certified lenders are banks and non-banks that participate in the SBA loan program on a regular basis and are involved with the SBA training and certification. A longer processing time can be experienced with certified lenders since the loan must still be reviewed and approved by the SBA, although the turnaround time has been reduced to 3 to 5 days.

Participant lenders make SBA loans on an infrequent basis. The disadvantage of this type of lender — and this category includes the majority of banks and non-bank lenders — is that after the loan has been approved by the lender, it still must be reviewed and approved by the SBA. This not only takes longer, but also opens the door for further scrutiny by the SBA loan analyst who has not had any personal contact with you, the borrower.

SBA LOAN DOCUMENTATION

Any SBA lender will require the following information when considering a loan request.

For new businesses:

1. The SBA Application Form, which describes the loan amount and purpose of the loan.

2. The background and roles of key managers and the owners.

3. Personal financial statements and income tax returns for two years.

4. Projection of profit and loss and cash flow statements for two years.

5. The list of any available collateral.

6. The business plan.

For existing businesses:

1. Income tax returns for the last three years.

2. Income statements for the last three years.

3. Personal financial statements of the owners.

4. A list of the collateral available.

5. The business plan.

ADVANTAGES AND DISADVANTAGES OF SBA LOANS

> **Secret:** The "advantages" far outweigh the "disadvantages."

When considering SBA loans, be aware of the advantages and disadvantages.

Some of the advantages are:

1. **The longer maturity.** Through the SBA loan program, a business can obtain a working capital loan for up to 7 years, equipment loans for up to 10 years and real estate loans for up to 25 years. These repayment programs are much more liberal than a conventional bank loan. Another advantage is that the real estate loans only require a 10 percent down payment, as compared to the 20-25 percent down payment usually required.

2. **Competitive interest rates.** SBA loan rates are usually lower than conventional loan rates because of the reduction in risk to the banks based on the SBA's guarantee.

3. **Capital leverage.** Most banks are limited to making loans to companies that have a debt-to-worth ratio of 2:1, while the SBA can go up to a 4:1 ratio.

4. **No prepayment penalty.** If your company is growing rapidly and you can either pay the loan off or need to finance for a larger amount, no additional payment will be assessed.

5. **Eligibility.** SBA loans emphasize the cash flow of the borrower and the company, and put less emphasis on collateral.

Collateral is obtained and required, but it becomes a secondary source.

6. **Collateral.** Because of the SBA guarantees, a wider range of collateral can be used to secure a loan, such as jewelry, antiques, paintings and rare coins. Banks don't accept this type of collateral, which is referred to as pawn shop collateral.

The disadvantages of SBA loans include:

1. **Collateral.** Applicants are often surprised when the lender requires that the loan be secured in addition to the SBA guarantee.

2. **Paperwork.** Although the red tape and bureaucracy has been reduced substantially through the LODOC program and other efficiencies, there is without question more paperwork required than for a regular bank loan.

3. **Negative covenants.** In exchange for the SBA guaranteeing your business loan, the agency might put limits on how much you spend for salaries and certain capital improvements without getting prior approval.

4. **Longer process.** If you do not use a preferred lender, you will have to go through the qualification process twice, since the bank will have to submit the loan to the SBA again after it has been approved internally.

FREE MANAGEMENT ASSISTANCE PROGRAMS

The SBA believes that the primary reason for most small business failures is poor management. Because of this, the agency has set up management training programs to assist small businesses in the areas of finance, marketing, human resources and other key areas of running a small business. These programs are presented through colleges, chambers of commerce and different business associations in the form of individual counseling, SBA-sponsored courses, conferences, workshops and publications.

Secret: The SBDC and SCORE are probably the best resources available to small businesses from start-ups to growing businesses. THEIR ASSISTANCE IS FREE!!!!

Business assistance is provided primarily through the Service Corps of Retired Executives, or SCORE, through Small Business Institutes, known as SBIs, and Small Business Development Centers, known as SBDCs and other associations. SCORE is staffed by more than 14,000 retired executives who provide management consulting to small businesses; SBA matches the background of the SCORE volunteer with the individual needs of the business owner. The advantage of SCORE counseling is that it is a free service from seasoned and experienced entrepreneurs. The disadvantage is that a great majority of the former and retired executives are not up-to-date on current technological advances and assistance that can help the small business owner.

The SBI is a cooperative program with the SBA and more than 600 colleges and universities around the country. SBI sites provide senior and graduate students who work with small businesses under the guidance of their faculty advisors. The small business owner benefits from this free consulting while the students benefit from the real-life experience of working in a business.

SBDCs also use the resources of colleges and universities in conjunction with local, state and federal programs to provide one-on-one management training and technical assistance to small businesses from experts in their respective fields. This service is also free.

See the Resource Guide at the back of this book for the location and phone number for the nearest SBDC office, or call 703-448-6124.

ASSISTANCE FOR WOMEN-OWNED BUSINESSES

In addition to the SBA programs, the following organizations assist women in their businesses:

1. **The Association of Enterprise Opportunities** provides a list of micro lenders in your region. Contact AEO at 320 North Michigan Avenue, Suite 804, Chicago, IL 60601.

2. **The National Association of Women Business Advocates** provides initiative and supports women business owners. Contact the Ohio Department of Development, 77 South High Street, Columbus, OH 43255.

3. **The Office of Women Business Ownership** provides the latest information on federal loans and other programs for women. Contact the Business Women's Ownership, SBA Central Office, 409 3rd Street, Washington, DC 20416.

4. **Compass Rose** offers training and financial support programs for female entrepreneurs. Contact the Compass Rose Corporation at 20 Moore's Road, Frazer, PA 19355.

See the Resource Guide at the back of this book for more programs and information.

LOCAL AND STATE PROGRAMS

There are numerous state, county and municipal programs being developed to meet the needs of those businesses that do not qualify for traditional bank financing or federal assistance.

1. **Community Development Corporations**, also known as CDCs,

receive grants from both state and federal government sources
to finance businesses in economically depressed areas where
unemployment is running high. CDCs specialize in start-up
businesses and those that will create the largest number of jobs
per investment dollar. CDCs have a great deal of flexibility in
structuring the loan and collateral requirements. Loans can
run up to $500,000, repayable over 10 years.

In addition to loans, CDC Services will also provide assistance
in analyzing and preparing your financial projections and
gathering and interpreting data about your target market.
They will also assist in finding and developing plant sites and
providing generalized business counseling.

2. **The Economic Development Agency** of your county and city
   can help you locate information on programs set up to assist
   start-ups and small businesses. These loan programs, referred
   to as GAP loans and micro-loan programs (for loans of less
   than $10,000), are run in conjunction with local banks, where
   the loan initially originates. If the applicant is deficient in the
   areas of collateral, repayment, cash flow, etc., but the bank is
   willing to make the loan because of a strong interest in this
   type of business, the lender will approach the local municipal
   or county economic development to fund the remaining balance of the loan.

For the nearest Community Development Corporation in your
area, see the Resource Guide in the back of this book, or phone 202-
293-7587. To locate the offices in your particular area for state loan
programs and grants, contact the Economic Development Agency at
the state level.

Another resource for local and state financial programs is the
World Wide Web. Check each state's Web site — addresses are listed

in the Resource Guide at the back of this book — for the programs available and links to cities you are interested in.

GOVERNMENT GRANTS

In addition to making loans, the federal government and the SBA are involved with making grants, which do not have to be paid back. Almost every department in the federal government has grant money at some time or another. The most successful grant program is called the Small Business Innovation Research Program, designed to support advances in research in the scientific and engineering areas and to encourage conversion of research and development from government and military uses into commercial applications. These grants range from $50,000 to $500,000.

To contact the Small Business Innovative Research Program, phone 202-653-6458.

> *Far better it is to dare mighty things, to win glorious triumphs, even though checkered by failure, than to take rank with those poor spirits who neither enjoy much nor suffer much, because they live in the gray twilight that knows not victory nor defeat.*
>
> THEODORE ROOSEVELT

3

BANKS AND BANKERS

*Banks are where you get the money only after you have
proven that you don't need it.*

BOB HOPE

OVERVIEW

IN THIS CHAPTER, WE'LL LOOK AT THE EXPECTATIONS OF THE DECISION-makers who will act on your application for financing. We'll talk about dealing with banks and bankers and share some inside tips on how to nurture that important banking relationship. We will discuss the four types of commercial loans and how to determine which is best for your company's needs, and the six key elements that need to be addressed in order to get a loan request approved. We will also outline the famous "5C's" test used by bankers to analyze your loan request and the questions most often asked by bankers during the loan interview.

> **Secret:** Very few companies have grown successfully without a solid banking relationship.

BANKS DON'T MAKE LOANS

It's important to realize that banks don't make loans; bankers do. There is a difference. Banks are large institutions with bureaucratic red tape. Bankers are individuals like you and me who are subject to the same likes and dislikes as the rest of us.

One of the key components to finding a lender who understands your business is to deal with a loan officer who is at least a vice president or above. Previous experience is a key factor in a banker's willingness to take risks. A junior loan officer is more concerned about making a bad loan — and a bad impression on the higher-ups — than a seasoned loan officer.

Bankers, junior and senior, are sometimes guilty of using the baby-with-the-bathwater analysis when looking at loan requests. For example, if the banker or the bank has recently sustained a serious loss on a business in the health-care field, it will be very difficult to overcome this negative experience if your business is also in the health-care field. Although it has nothing to do with you, your business might get a better reception at another institution.

Money talks but it never debates.

GETTING TO KNOW YOUR BANKER

Given all that, where does one begin in nurturing the banker, and what are some of the things that work and what are some of the things that should be avoided in developing that relationship? Before we discuss that, ask yourself a few questions to see if you are a candidate for improving and nurturing your banking relationship.

1. Do you know where your banker grew up, his home town, where he went to school, what he majored in? Do you know anything about his family, brothers, sisters, spouse, children? What are the banker's favorite sports? What interests is he involved in outside the bank?

2. Have you gone out socially with your banker during the last 12 months? Did you invite your banker to the company Christmas party or picnic? Did you give your banker a small Christmas gift last year, something under $25 and preferably non-alcoholic? With most bankers, the traditional bottle of "Christmas cheer" has a negative effect. Much better is a gift, such as a book about the banker's hobby or interest, that shows that you thought about the banker as a person during the holiday season. The banker does not look upon such a gift as bribery or trying to buy influence; it's taken as an expression of a personal thought.

3. Have you taken your banker on a tour of your facility to point out improvements in the plant and equipment during the last six months? Have you referred, or better yet, introduced another customer to your banker in the last 12 months? Does your banker know your attorney and accountant by name?

4. Do you know the name of your banker's boss? And, more importantly, do you know the banker's lending limit — and the banker's boss's lending limit — before you have to go to the loan committee?

What do these types of questions have to do with getting a loan? Everything. When you can answer these questions "yes," what you are doing is establishing that important relationship with the banker. You have to have that relationship established with the banker before he or she feels comfortable with the loan.

Even if you're not a banker, you can probably understand that it is a lot easier to deal with and to honor requests from people we enjoy and relate to. It's much more difficult to turn down a request from someone we enjoy and have respect for. It's also much easier to turn down a request from someone you really don't know and haven't established a relationship with, and only comes to you when they need something.

You have to remember, bankers are people, too, and they want to be liked, they really do. They've got a job to do and they've got lots of regulations to deal with. But, if you keep that in mind, you'll see how critical establishing that relationship is to the overall lending process.

STARTING A RELATIONSHIP BEFORE YOU'RE STRAPPED FOR CASH

Secret: A common denominator of poor decisions is "snap judgments." Bankers are trained to take their time in analyzing a loan request in order to obtain more and more information.

It sounds odd, but the key to nurturing or establishing a banking relationship is showing the banker that you do not need the money today. The best time to approach the banker is **when you do not need a loan**.

It's much more effective for you, the borrower, to start out by saying, "I don't need a loan today, but if the business continues to grow as my accountant or my financial planner is projecting, we're going to be needing some capital down the road to fund this additional growth." Bankers love that.

The worst time to be establishing a banking relationship is when you do need the loan today. It takes your negotiating power completely off the table and puts the banker on the defensive.

The absolutely worst type of loan requests come on Friday at 3 p.m. — and they do come in. The bank has a $150,000 loan out to a company; the owner calls and says, "Harold, I need to have $10,000 put in our checking account immediately to cover payroll. If not we're going to have to shut down and you'll just have to come in and take over the plant and the equipment on Monday." These are phone calls that can wreck any relationship that might have existed between the business owner and the banker before the phone call.

Even if you are getting your funding from an outside source, it is critical to have a banking relationship established for future needs. If nothing else, your commercial checking account can be used as a reference in obtaining credit from suppliers. It is much more effective to give suppliers an actual person to talk to, as in, "Call Mr. Jones at First National Bank," when they ask for the name of your banker.

HAVING A BACKUP BANKER

> **Secret:** Don't put all of your financial "eggs" in one basket.

In today's ever-changing financial world with bank mergers and acquisitions, it is becoming imperative to establish a secondary or backup banking relationship, one that can be implemented immediately, if necessary. Some of the following suggestions apply not only to existing businesses, but also to start-up businesses that are going to need to nurture or establish a primary banking relationship.

When establishing a secondary or backup banking relationship, let the banker know that you're pleased with your present banking relationship, but that your accountant, financial planner or your advisory board has suggested that you establish a backup banking relationship as a prudent business practice. These are very, very positive statements to the banker, letting him or her know that you're planning ahead and that you don't need the money today, it's not a last minute, fill-in-the-gap situation.

ASKING FOR REFERRALS

One of the necessary first steps in establishing or nurturing that banking relationship is to talk to your friends, your associates, social contacts, other businesses that you deal with. Ask them for the name of a banker they have enjoyed working with and that they could refer you to.

This serves two purposes:

1. It serves as a screening device to locate an aggressive banker because the people you're asking are going to be friends or people who know you on a personal basis. They're not going to be referring you to someone who has been unfair or hard to deal with.

2. When you call the banker for the appointment, you are going to use that person's name as a referral. It helps tremendously in getting your foot in the door by using the customer's name.

After you've obtained the names of several bankers, try to get a mix of several of the large chain banks and a couple of the local independent banks. Four seems to be an ideal number.

SETTING THE APPOINTMENT

You then call the respective banks and ask for the secretary to the banker you are calling. Very important. Don't call for the banker directly. Call for the secretary. The secretary controls this banker's life and screens everything.

It's also very important that you get to know the secretary and be as friendly as you can. Let the secretary know early in the conversation that the bank's customer, John Jones, has recommended that you talk to this banker to discuss your business and that you want to make an appointment. That will get you in the door without a problem because bankers are very sensitive to bad publicity, and if someone referred you to them, that carries a lot of weight.

DRESSING APPROPRIATELY

When you meet with the banker, dress appropriately, that is, appropriate for your profession. If you're a carpenter or a contractor, don't wear a three-piece suit, silk shirt and silk tie. That's not the look the banker expects from someone who is supposedly out in the field doing work. Dress neatly, and appropriately for your profession.

TAKING CONTROL

> **Secret:** One has to realize early that negotiating with the banker is NOT played on a "level playing field." Think about the last time you visited the bank. The atmosphere is intimidating: you walk past an armed security guard, who seems to be scrutinizing you; video cameras are everywhere; huge steel doors and bars are in the vault area; the banker's oversized desk keeps distance between you and the banker; and the overstuffed chair that faces the banker makes you feel like the banker is looking "down" at you.

When you introduce yourself to the banker, share two things right off the bat:

1. You are interviewing several banks in the area to establish your account or a secondary banking relationship with, and this bank was recommended by a customer, John Jones. Put the banker in a position where he or she is going to have to sell the

bank to you because you're looking at several competitors. You have the added bonus of being referred by a customer, someone who knows the bank. This is a very effective door-opener and is the beginning of leveling the playing field with the banker.

2. You're not here today to seek a loan, but you're meeting with different bankers to find a mutually beneficial banking relationship. You're looking for a bank that can handle your present needs and also be able to handle your future needs if you continue to grow according to your projections for present sales levels. Very positive things for you to be communicating to the banker.

Let the banker know that you are aware that the schedule is tight, but you do have a couple of questions before leaving a business plan for him or her to read at his or her convenience. At this point, you have endeared yourself to the banker by recognizing that he or she is short on time.

It also gives you a good reason not to present the business plan at the outset. If you do, the banker will pick it up and start reading it while you're talking. You don't want that document to be reviewed while you are trying to sell yourself and your company. You want the banker's undivided attention. This is a very critical time of establishing that banking relationship. So save the business plan for the end of the meeting and you'll stay in control of the situation.

ASKING QUESTIONS

Secret: Make the banker sell themselves and the bank to you.

Some of the questions you might want to ask the banker:

1. What is the banker's or bank's experience and feelings about businesses in your particular industry or service? Is it something they have had good or bad loan experience with? Or is this one area where they haven't had any experience at all? You want to hear about how interested and knowledgeable they are about your business.

2. How long has the loan officer been with the bank?

3. What is the bank's "CAMEL" rating? This is an acronym for a system that has been used by federal and state regulatory agencies in recent years to rate the bank's performance, much like Moody's rating for the bond market. It covers five separate categories:

   ◆ Capital

   ◆ Assets

   ◆ Management

   ◆ Earnings

   ◆ Liquidity

   These five separate categories are rated from 1 to 5: 1 being excellent, 5 representing a serious problem. A composite of scores in the five areas gives the bank an overall rating between 1 and 5. This is public information, and asking for it is a good, effective way of letting the banker know that you are not only interested in obtaining a loan, but you're interested in doing business with someone who is going to be around tomorrow.

   If the banker hesitates about giving you this information, you can bet the bank's rating must be in the 4 to 5 range. If it's in the 1 or 2 category, they are going to be very proud of sharing that information with you. In the 3 category, they might hem and haw a little bit, but this is important information, because you want to be dealing with a bank that is on sound footing.

You can also obtain a credit rating report on a bank by calling either VeriBank, 1-800-442-2657 or Sheshunoff Information Services, 1-512-472-2244. The cost for the reports is $10 for the first bank and $5 for each additional bank requested.

4. What are the bank's procedures for any loan requests in the future? You need to know if you are going to be working with this loan officer or if your request is something that has to go to the loan committee. This is a very tactful way of finding out what the loan officer's lending limit is and if you're going to need to nurture the loan officer's boss, too, since you want the largest number of people on your side in that loan committee. If you can avoid having your loan go before the dreaded loan committee, all the better, because to the people you've not established a relationship with on the loan committee, you're just a piece of paper. It is very easy to turn down those loan requests.

5. What additional information will the bank need in addition to your business plan? What do they want from you in addition to income tax returns? Do they want projections for three to five years, or do they want to see an accounts receivable aging? What is the normal turnaround time once these items are submitted before you get a decision?

At the end of the meeting, hand the loan officer your business plan, and ask when you can get back in touch to answer any questions. The banker will always have questions on the business plan, if only to show you he has read it and how smart he is. They love to impress you and try to test your knowledge about the business in the business plan.

When we pray for rain, we must be willing to put up with some mud.

VISITING THE NEW ACCOUNTS DEPARTMENT

Secret: Now you will start "tilting" the banker's "playing field" in your favor. This is where the fun begins!

Before you leave the loan officer's desk, ask for directions to the new accounts department. This sends a positive message to the banker that you're interested or you would not be asking for information on new accounts. Most of the time, the banker will take you over personally to the new accounts department and introduce you.

Establishing a depository account is a very sensitive and important part of a banking relationship; it is very important to the banker that the bank get not only the loan, but also the depository relationship. The depository accounts are the source of funding for new loans, the new inventory that enables the bank to make a profit.

You won't be spending very much time in the new accounts area, just long enough to describe the type of business that you have and ask for recommendations on the type of account and services to meet your needs. Before you leave you want to get a copy of the brochure that describes the services along with the cost, so you can study them at a later time.

The other thing you want to ask for — and this is an absolute must — is any free item they are giving to customers, such as pens, matches, calendars, mugs inscribed with "I had coffee with the president of ABC Bank," anything that has the bank's name on it. Don't be shy; they love to give this stuff away.

Now that you have this "stuff," take it back to the office and put it away. You'll need it later.

CALLING THE BANKERS BACK

After you have interviewed four banks, you should be able to select the two that seem to show the most interest and that you feel the most comfortable with. Contact the bankers you spoke to and ask if they have any questions about your business plan. Answer the bankers' questions directly and confidently. If you don't know the answer, don't guess. Let the bankers know that you would like to research that question and get back to them, because you want to make sure that you are accurate.

Bankers respect hearing that as opposed to someone who tries to "shoot from the hip." It gives them a very uncomfortable feeling when someone doesn't take the time to get the right information. There is nothing wrong with saying "I don't know the answer, but let me get with my accountant, or my sales marketing people to get you a more definite answer."

You also want to tell the bankers that you are going to keep them posted of the progress of your business by dropping off monthly profit and loss statements so they can keep updated on your progress.

BRINGING THE BANKERS HOME

Secret: It is important to get the banker on your "turf." It is very difficult to develop the relationship with the banker on the banker's "turf."

You now want to invite each banker to your facility for a tour of the business. Remember the "stuff" from all of the banks that you have visited? Take out the items you picked up from a competing bank and place them in appropriate, strategic positions around your office. For example, put a wall calendar off to one side behind your desk. Put the matches off to another side of the desk; pens in a naturally visible area; fill the mug with coffee.

This is where you will have fun watching the eyes of the banker as you're talking about your business. As you look down, just look up very quickly. The banker's eyes will be on that calendar or those matches or those pens, getting the message, "Oh, no! Our competitor has been out here trying to hustle this account, too. This must be a highly sought-after business. Just look at all the stuff around here."

Psychologically, when more than one person is after something, there is competition. This is another way of leveling that banking playing field so that when you are ready to ask for a loan, the lender is ready to listen.

Types Of Loans

There are four types of commercial loans.

1. **A single payment loan.** It is usually for one year or less and used for a particular purpose, such as to take a large discount on an early payment of large purchase, or to fund cash flow on a temporary basis when there is excess inventory.

2. **The installment loan.** This is made on monthly payments for a set period of time and is usually secured with machinery, equipment, automobiles, trucks, computers and other types of depreciating assets.

3. **A term loan.** This is for a multi-year period and payable on a monthly or quarterly basis from cash flow. It is used to fund long-term expansion programs.

4. **The revolving line of credit.** This is a type of loan that provides a source of funds set at a certain amount on which you, the

borrower, can draw down when the cash flow is running low and pay back at your convenience when the cash flow improves. These types of lines of credit are usually set up for seasonal purposes, or to even out monthly cash flow.

It is important to match the type of loan with a source of repayment. If the payment is going to be coming from a single, identifiable source, it should be a short-term loan. If the funds to repay the loan are to be coming out of profits or cash flow over a period of time, the loan should be a long-term loan. Most companies have a combination of two or more commercial loans to match the funding source with the needs.

WHAT BANKERS LOOK AT

When evaluating your loan request, bankers generally look at six different areas:

1. **Quality of management.** Quality of management is determined by previous experience dealing with challenging situations as a manager or owner of a business. It is not absolutely necessary to have experience in a particular industry. It is more important to have demonstrated the ability to deal with challenges and successfully turn a problem situation into a positive one. An example would be to show that as a manager of a department of your previous employer or company you were able to improve the profit margin from 10 percent to 30 percent, or to reduce employee turnover from 10 percent down to 1 percent. What the banker is trying to determine is your ability to deal with the continuing challenges that face the small business. Bankers are not comfortable with someone who will hope that a problem will go away. They are looking more for a person who will take the bull by the horns and deal with the situation immediately.

2. **The accounting system.** Specifically, does it provide accurate information? If the pro-formas or the financial statements are not presented using standard accounting format, the banker feels very uncomfortable with the quality and credibility of the numbers. An example of this would be a company's balance sheet which does not depreciate for fixed assets.

3. **Market trends for the product or service that the small business is providing.** Bankers feel more comfortable with growth trends that are supported with outside independent research and articles showing that this is a growth industry for the next five to seven years, not a buggy-whip industry that is either obsolete or in a state of decline. The banker feels, no matter how good the management is, if the market trends are negative, it's very much like swimming upstream.

4. **Structure of management and ownership.** Bankers realize it is very difficult for the owner to be a specialist in all aspects of operating a business: finance, marketing and human resources. Bankers feel very comfortable with people who acknowledge and realize that there are certain areas they are stronger in than others. What steps is the owner taking to bring in assistance or to outsource those functions in which he or she is not strong? Bankers like to see owners who are self-confident but also realistic in the areas where they need assistance. Bankers also love to see companies set up advisory boards that meet twice a year or more.

5. **Profitability.** Bankers have moved away from looking at collateral as a main source of repaying loans and are looking more at the cash flow and cash flow projections of the company. Banks' previous experience selling collateral and realizing only five to ten cents on the dollar has forced them to abandon their traditional priorities.

6. **The company's pro-forma profit and loss statements and the cash flow statements and projections.** The banker is especially interested in the assumptions that provide support for a sudden increase in sales or a sudden decrease in operating expenses.

THE "5C'S" TEST

Secret: Although banking has become more sophisticated in the past few years, the "5C's Test" is still the foundation of lending decisions.

Small business owners often hear of the famous "5C's." The "5C's" that bankers use in testing the company represent:

♦ Character

♦ Capacity

♦ Conditions

♦ Collateral

♦ Capital

1. **Character** comes first on the list, because bankers feel very uncomfortable if this element is missing. They are able to assess the character issue through referrals and determining the honesty of the individual in previous situations and business dealings with other clients.

   They are also able to ascertain the character of an individual by taking a look at the personal financial statement and determining if the owner is conservative by keeping a percentage of assets in liquidity. A banker feels very uncomfortable seeing a non-liquid statement, especially if the assets are "toys" such as boats, recreational vehicles, mountain property, speculative investments, etc.

The banker will also get a feel for the character of the person through conversations in which the customer reveals priorities for the business. The customer who brags to the banker about avoiding taxes by understating income leaves the banker wondering what else the person is doing that might be misleading.

2. **Capacity** is how you have dealt with problems and challenges in the past. Bankers have found that poor business judgment can be a major cause of failure. Bankers like to know that the borrower understands how cash moves through the company and how poor credit policies and poor collection policies can adversely affect the cash flow and the integrity of the company.

The banker understands, and expects the business owner to comprehend, that sales is not the paramount answer to a successful company. The banker also expects the borrower to understand the factors necessary to be successful. The banker wants to make sure that the borrower has a clear focus on why his product or service is better than that of competitors. The banker is looking for the borrower to acknowledge and understand the risks associated with his particular business, and any contingency plans that the company has put in place if the economy faces a downturn, or if a new competitor enters the market.

3. **Conditions** are the external factors facing the company, such as the present economy of the local area and also the national market if the product or service is sold outside the local area.

4. **Collateral** has moved behind cash flow in importance but is still taken as supplemental support for the loan. The value placed on the collateral is what the banker feels it can be sold for in a distressed situation, and the business owner should not be taken back by such a low figure. The borrower can play a key role in educating the banker as to the true market value of specialized equipment and collateral by providing appraisals and letters from buyers and suppliers of this type of merchandise.

5. **Capital** is the "blood equity" invested by the owner in the business. Banks are very conservative lenders and will not make a 100 percent capital loan to start a business. One of the key criteria in the loan decision is how much the owner would stand to lose if the business were to fail. The greater amount of investment or blood equity on the part of the owner, the greater the chances the loan will be approved.

WHAT BANKERS ASK

Secret: Bankers love to ask questions. "He who holds the gold, makes the rules." The questions are intended not only to obtain needed information about you and your company, but also to judge your management style, i.e., do you acknowledge when you don't have the answer to their question or are you one that always "shoots from the hip?" Very important to acknowledge when you don't know the answer to their question BUT that you will research the question and get back with them in the next few days. This wins points with bankers.

Although each banker has different requirements, there are several questions that most bankers will always ask. And when the banker asks, you, the borrower, must be completely straightforward with your answers.

Secret: There are two "schools" of thought on how much to seek from the bank. I recommend requesting a smaller amount in order to get your "foot" in the door of the bank.

1. **How much money do you want?** This might seem like a very basic question but it is important, since there are two schools of thought on the amount of loan to request. One says to obtain the largest loan you can possibly get. The other says to go for the minimum loan that will get you through the first six to nine months of operation while you build your relationship and track record with the banker.

It is much easier to obtain the second loan from the banker if you can demonstrate a successful track record in meeting or exceeding your projections. You are also cutting down your chances for rejection since it is much easier to get a loan for $50,000 than one for $100,000. The higher the loan amount, the greater the chance of the bank taking a loss. This is just part of the banker's personality, so with a lower loan amount there's also a lower threshold of potential loss in the mind of the banker.

It is much easier and acceptable to the banking institution to come in six to nine months later with an additional loan request to support a growing business. It is much more difficult to try to get that commitment prior to establishing that important relationship with the banker and a track record to support the larger loan amount.

2. **What you are going to do with the money?** Again, this sounds very basic, but often a borrower is evasive and fails to identify the benefits of the loan to the business. Be specific in identifying that the loan is going to be used to purchase a temporary increase in inventory that you were able to pick up at a low price which will be repaid from the turnover of receivables, or to purchase a machine which will increase productivity and thus reduce your operating costs by 15 percent to 20 percent.

3. **What are the benefits to your company of borrowing additional funds and taking the additional risk?** The benefits need to be clearly spelled out in terms of profit, market penetration, additional product lines or stabilization of customer base.

4. **When will the loan be repaid?** This is very important, because there are several types of loans and it is important that *you* be in control of the type that will be ultimately undertaken. Don't rely on the bankers to make this decision for you. The bank would like to have your loan paid back yesterday.

    The key determining factor is the source of repayment. If it's going to come within a short time, within one year, it can be a single payment loan. If it's going to require payment from cash flow, it should be a term loan spread out over several years. Don't make the mistake of trying to repay a capital loan with short-term working capital proceeds.

5. **How is the loan going to be repaid?** Are we talking about cash flow, which would repay a long term capital loan? Are we talking about the turnover of inventory and receivables and a leveling off of inventory, which will allow excess cash to reduce the loan? Or are we talking about refinancing from another financing source? Are we talking about initial investors injecting money into the company to repay the loan?

6. **What are your contingency plans in case something happens so the loan cannot be repaid on schedule?** What steps are *you* as a business owner going to take, such as reducing inventory, reducing operating costs, reducing overhead? What is it going to take to generate the funds necessary to repay the bank loan?

FOLLOWING UP

> **Secret:** This seemingly small gesture will elevate you from the rest of the banker's commercial clients. Extremely effective in developing the important relationship with the banker.

Once you have been able to negotiate a loan with the banker, don't forget to send a personal thank-you note. And one to the banker's boss, letting the boss know how professional the loan officer was in dealing with your loan request, and that you will recommend the bank to your business associates. This might seem like a small and subtle thing to do, but bankers really do cherish these rare acknowledgments of appreciation.

> *You can get anything in life you want, if you help*
> *enough people get what they want.*
>
> ZIG ZIGLAR

4

FUNDING SOURCES: NON-BANK ALTERNATIVES

Persistence will give you power to prevail over all problems.

OVERVIEW

IN THIS CHAPTER, WE WILL BE TALKING ABOUT THE USE OF NON-BANK sources such as accounts receivable, factoring, inventory financing, lease financing and real estate financing. We'll also look at how to choose alternative financing for your business.

ACCOUNTS RECEIVABLE FINANCING

Secret: This is one of the fastest growing areas of money sources for most businesses. It has gotten very competitive and costs have dropped in recent years. Don't overlook this growing source of funding.

Accounts receivable means the money owed to your company for the sale of merchandise or services to your customers. Accounts receivable can be an excellent source of financing if your customers are creditworthy. The nice thing about accounts receivable financing is that the lender is basing the decision not so much on the strength of you, the borrower, but upon the credit strength and financial strength of your customers.

Your first choice for obtaining accounts receivable financing should be a commercial bank, because the costs are the lowest. You will need to contact the larger commercial banks in your area to see if they are set up to handle accounts receivable financing; some specialize in this area.

The procedures for obtaining accounts receivable financing are similar to those for other types of loans, except for some additional reporting to keep the lender informed of the status of the collection of the accounts. You are usually required to send a lender a weekly report based upon the payments you received and any new receivables that have been created from new sales.

As the payments are collected they are applied to the loan on the same percentage basis that the bank is advancing on the receivables, usually 70 to 80 percent. The remaining amount collected from your customers then goes into your account.

FACTORING — ADVANTAGES AND DISADVANTAGES

Factoring is another way of utilizing accounts receivable to raise cash. The cost of having a non-bank company that specializes only in collection of accounts receivable is more expensive, but the paperwork and time-frame to obtain approval is much shorter than a commercial bank.

There are certain advantages and disadvantages of factoring.

Advantages:

1. **You receive immediate cash once you have received the purchase invoice of a customer.**

2. **Reduced cost of collecting the receivables.** The factoring company is responsible for collecting all moneys from the customer. This eliminates the need to have a staff person in your company doing the bookkeeping, credit collection and follow-up work on these accounts.

3. **The accounting and collection knowledge of the factor is very strong.** Since the factor will be keeping the accounting records on a daily basis, you will have access to instant verification and status reports of your customers' accounts.

Disadvantages:

1. **Depending on the creditworthiness of your customers, the factor may make the accounts receivable commitment on a recourse basis.** This means that if the factor is unable to collect the full amount from the customer for any reason, the factor will look to you, the borrower, to reimburse him for the difference.

2. **Notifying your customers to send payments to a post office box instead of directly to your company.** This is the factor's way of controlling the receivables and having immediate collection and notification of any potential problems. Some businesses are sensitive to having their customers notified that they are using a factor for their financing. However, as the banking and financial industry has changed and factoring has become more popular over the last five to seven years, this disadvantage is rapidly disappearing.

3. **The cost of using a factor is higher than a commercial bank.** It can run between 5 percent and 15 percent discount based

upon the quality, dollar amount and number of invoices being processed. (That means that when you receive payment from your customers, the factor will keep 5 to 15 percent of the payment and deposit the balance in your account.) The larger the dollar amount, the fewer the invoices and the higher the quality of the customer, the lower the cost of factoring. Factors look at not only the financial strength of the customer, but also that of the borrower and the type of industry that the customer is in.

It is important to take a look at the total picture and balance both the costs and benefits of factoring, since some companies have experienced a large savings in the collection on accounts receivable by using factors.

You can locate factors in your area by looking in the Yellow Pages under "Factors."

INVENTORY FINANCING

Although inventory financing is somewhat limited since lenders also want accounts receivables that accompany the inventory's collateral, there are certain companies that specialize in making loans secured by inventory.

There are two types of inventory financing:

1. Floor planning

2. Warehouse financing.

Floor planning is usually done by the dealer selling the inventory, such as an automobile dealer.

Warehouse financing is usually done by an outside company that monitors the inventory by bonding one of your own employees to keep track of what is sold and new merchandise that arrives. This way, the warehouse control company knows how much collateral is present on the premises on any given day.

This form of financing can be expensive, depending upon the nature of the collateral. If the collateral is specialized or a seasonal type of merchandise, the risk that the lender will not be able to sell it to get the amount of the loan back is higher, and therefore the costs are higher. If the merchandise is universally used and not seasonal, the costs of inventory financing are reduced substantially.

LEASE FINANCING

Secret: Both the processing time and paperwork are much less than the bank's requirements.

The three main sources of lease financing are:

1. General equipment

2. Specialized equipment

3. Vendor financing.

General equipment leasing companies are not limited to one particular type of equipment on which they will provide financing. These companies handle both new and used equipment.

Specialized equipment lenders deal with high-dollar types of equipment; they have developed a reputation for being able to sell the specialized equipment to a secondary market in case of repossession or sale at the end of the lease term. Companies in this area usually deal with aircraft, medical equipment, construction equipment, large computer systems and dry cleaning equipment.

Vendor financing is when the seller of the equipment has a captive leasing company or an arrangement with a leasing company to facilitate the financing on the equipment. There are usually side agreements with the seller of the equipment that any equipment will be resold by the dealer if it is repossessed or turned in at the end of the lease term. The vendors have a better access to a secondary market of buyers for this used equipment than would other lenders, such as banks.

The advantage of vendor financing to you, the company, is one-stop shopping. Providing lease financing on-site greatly increases sales if customers do not have to go out and find their own financing. It is definitely a sales enhancer.

ADVANTAGES AND REQUIREMENTS OF LEASING

> **Secret:** This area of financing has become very creative in the past five years. Remember to acquire appreciating assets and lease depreciating assets.

Advantages of leasing include:

1. No capital investment or down payment on the equipment. This is very important for new or growing companies that can better utilize their funds in purchasing inventory which turns over much quicker and produces a greater profit.

2. You can get out of a leasing agreement when the equipment is technologically out-of-date or of no use to you and your business at the end of the lease.

3. You can also have a maintenance contract incorporated in the lease payments, so that someone else is responsible for the maintenance and upkeep of the leased equipment.

4. There are also tax benefits to leasing equipment which should be discussed with your accountant.

5. Leasing can also turn equipment that is already owned by your company into instant cash. This can be created with a

sale/lease-back arrangement, in which you temporarily sell your equipment for immediate cash, then lease the equipment back for two to five years.

There are several general requirements for leasing:

1. Some type of business plan that provides the information the leasing company will need to access the market and the type of customers you will be dealing with.

2. The cash flow projections and cash flow statements of the business. Like a bank, leasing companies are interested in the ability of the company to generate enough cash flow to make the payments, rather than to liquidate the assets for cash.

3. The obsolescence factor. How quickly is equipment being replaced by new technology and improved performance? Computers are a good example of the rapid obsolescence factor incorporated in the cost of leasing. On the other hand, the leasing of a commercial oven or forklift has very low obsolescence and therefore the costs are reduced.

4. If the lease is a sale/lease-back arrangement, how the proceeds will be used in the company and how leasing will help the company. The leasing company will want to know specifically if the proceeds will be used to purchase such things as additional inventory, or to make improvements in the plant and equipment which would result in higher productivity.

5. What type of maintenance procedures or policies are in place. The leasing company wants to insure that the equipment will not be subject to excessive wear during the course of the lease.

6. The credit history of the company. The leasing company is concerned how the money is going to be repaid, and a previous credit history that demonstrates current payment is highly sought after and preferred.

REAL ESTATE FINANCING

An ideal source of financing for a start-up business is the use of real estate financing. You can use your own real estate as collateral, or the real estate of another person. The rule of thumb is that the lender will advance you 75 percent to 90 percent of the *net* equity of the property. Some aggressive lenders are offering loans up to 100 percent of net equity.

There are a number of sources for commercial real estate financing.

1. **Mortgage brokers and mortgage bankers** are firms that represent a number of different types of lenders specializing in different types of commercial real estate properties. They have a wide choice with regard to terms and rates based upon that particular lender's experience with that type of real estate.

2. **Savings and loans** specialize in real estate lending more so than the commercial banks. They have well-established secondary markets on to which they can sell the loans. However, the recent problems in the savings and loan industry have resulted in the consolidation of many institutions, leaving fewer in the marketplace.

3. **Banks** will make real estate commercial loans, but only if you are an established customer and if they have access to selling the loan off into a secondary market. Banks will often put a balloon payment on the loan within five to seven years since they are not specializing in long-term fixed rates.

4. **Life insurance companies** are also very active in commercial real estate. Their markets are usually the larger dollar properties of $1 million and above. It is the same with pension funds, although their loan floor limit is in the $250,000 range.

5. **Commercial finance companies** also make real estate loans on

commercial buildings, but their limit is usually $300,000 or less. Rates are slightly higher than other types of real estate lenders.

6. As a last resort, you can always obtain financing on commercial real estate properties by reviewing the Business Opportunity section in the newspaper under "Money to Loan." Of course, this source of money is very expensive, and should be used only as a last resort.

SHOPPING FOR ALTERNATIVE FINANCING

It is important when shopping for non-bank sources of financing to interview a number of different sources. Each seems to have its own unique policies and niches in the marketplace which also correlate to the cost.

When interviewing alternative funding sources, be prepared to discuss the following topics:

1. Information to show that the business is fairly stable and not subject to volatile changes.

2. The credit worthiness of your customers. Financially strong customers have more appeal than those of relatively new companies that have not established a credit history.

3. Factors also like to see a large customer base rather than just a few large customers, although they will make advances on single, large accounts receivable purchases based upon the credit-worthiness of the customer.

4. The average size of your receivables. Obviously, 100 accounts at $1,000 each are more attractive than 500 at $20 each.

5. The type of industry that you are in will be used to assess any particular problems you may face. For example, some indus-

tries such as construction and health care are notorious for slow pay, while restaurants are known for their instability.

With commercial real estate, you will have to shop the loan with several mortgage brokers to find the highest advance rating, best terms of repayment and lowest interest rates. Mortgage brokers will do all the leg work in locating the best lender to match your type of real estate and the terms and conditions you are seeking.

I would never have amounted to anything were it not for adversity. I was forced to come up the hard way.

J.C. PENNEY

5

BUYING AN EXISTING BUSINESS OR FRANCHISE

*The creation of something new is not accomplished by the
intellect but by the play instinct acting from inner
necessity. The creative mind plays with objects it loves.*

CARL G. JUNG

OVERVIEW

IN THIS CHAPTER WE WILL DISCUSS THE ADVANTAGES AND DISADVANtages of purchasing an existing business or franchise operation. We will see how you can blend your new, improved product or service with an existing business that handles similar products or services. We will also reveal the number one source of over 85 percent of the funding for the purchase of an existing business, and discuss some key items to look for in different franchises.

WHY BUY A BUSINESS?

By purchasing an existing business to add to your product or service

> **Secret:** Before you go full speed ahead with starting your own business, give some serious consideration to acquiring an existing business. The existing business should be one that is in the same industry as your new concept, but will allow you to add your product or service to an established market/clientele. It is easier than you think and the financing options are tremendous.

as opposed to starting a business from scratch you will greatly minimize the risk. You will also have available money sources start-ups could not tap.

Buying a business can be advantageous to two different groups of people.

1. **Those who have identified a particular market for a product or service.** By purchasing an existing business they will now be able to operate with very little change to the business in the future.

2. **Those who have identified a particular business or industry that they feel very comfortable with.** Through the introduction of additional products or services that complement and expand the existing product or service line to the same market, they can grow more rapidly.

SELLER FINANCING

> **Secret:** Seller financing is probably the least expensive and easiest financing available to acquire a business.

The main advantage for either one of these groups is that the seller will usually finance most of the purchase; in some cases up to 80 to

90 percent. In other words, the seller becomes the banker. This is a major stress reliever for a potential buyer, since dealing with the seller for the financing is much easier, faster and results in less brain damage than dealing with commercial banks or other traditional lenders.

But why wouldn't a seller want to sell the business only for cash and get on with his or her life?

ADVANTAGES TO THE SELLER

1. **There are very few potential buyers who can raise or borrow the full amount of the purchase price.** This cuts down tremendously on the market and affects the selling price, which will be reinforced by the business broker or agent listing the business for sale (who, by the way, is getting a commission based upon the selling price).

2. **Long-term capital gains tax,** which will allow the tax liability to be spread out over a number of years, in anticipation of lower capital-gains tax rates in the future.

3. **If the seller obtained all cash for the business, he'd be faced with the prospect of finding another investment.** It must have returns comparable to the rate of return on the seller carry-back note, with the same degree of risk. Not an easy thing to find these days.

ADVANTAGES TO THE BUYER

1. **The willingness of the seller to carry a note back on the sale of the business creates a great value in the eyes of the buyer.** It makes the buyer feel comfortable that the seller is not selling blue sky or a business likely to fail in the next several years

because of market conditions, competition, or information known only to the seller.

2. **Seller financing lets you use the profits of a company to buy yourself a job.**

3. **In the seller, you have a long-term expert who can be called upon in case there are any challenges or problems with the business.**

4. **In order to assure the payback of the note, the seller will be very cooperative in working with you in dealing with unforeseen problems,** and is much easier to deal with than a commercial bank or outside lenders. Sellers have often renegotiated the term, the interest rate and the amount of the carry-back note when the buyer has run into problems with the business, in order to protect the integrity of the note.

5. **Often, the interest rate is below commercial bank rates, with terms up to ten years.**

6. **Collateral is not an issue with the seller** since you are using the assets of the business as collateral for the loan. Only on rare occasions do sellers take personal collateral to secure the carry-back note, and this is usually associated with a lack of proven managerial experience on the part of the buyer.

7. **The mathematics of purchasing a business with seller financing are extremely attractive.** On the purchase of a $500,000 business it is much easier to accumulate personal funds and to utilize informal venture capitalists to come up with a $100,000 down payment, instead of $500,000 for the outright purchase of the business. It is much easier to convince other investors and lenders to advance the funds for the $100,000 down payment, even though you have little or no money invested in the

company, when the seller is willing to carry back 80 percent of the purchase price of an existing business with a proven cash flow.

BUYING A FRANCHISE

> **Secret:** When looking for the "right" franchise, many people overlook the basic rule of working, i.e., do something that you enjoy. When you are doing something that you enjoy, you are never working!

Purchasing a franchise can also be a ideal way of buying yourself a job with minimal personal cash investment.

The successful nature of franchising provides a formal training program based upon what has worked for previous franchises. Minimizing the possibility of repeating mistakes minimizes the chance for failure. The success rate with the majority of franchises runs in the 80 to 90 percent rate, which is very attractive to most investors.

ADVANTAGES OF FINANCING A FRANCHISE

1. **Most franchise companies have established banking relationships.** This helps facilitate establishing your own relationship with the bank when the franchiser has already opened the door for you.

2. **The lease financing of equipment is made available through previously arranged contacts with leasing companies by the franchiser at preferential rates.**

3. **It is much easier to get angels and other investors in a well-known franchise name.** There is comfort and security in know-

ing the success rate of other franchisees and being familiar with the name of the franchise.

4. **With any business, ultimately you are going to probably want to sell it.** It is much easier to sell a well-known name franchise than an individual company. Name recognition does count, and a premium is paid by the future buyer just has you paid a franchise fee.

5. **There is a full support team of technical and managerial systems to secure your success,** along with the camaraderie of other franchisees who can be called upon for their advice with any problems that might come up. This is a tremendous support system which is not available to the individual small business owner.

6. **A number of successful franchises do not require nor do they seek out previous experience in that particular industry.** They feel by not having preconceived ideas and habits, the franchise owner will more quickly learn and fit into the methods and philosophies of the franchiser.

LOCATING THE "RIGHT" FRANCHISE

Some key areas in evaluating the different franchises are:

1. How many years has a franchise been in business and how many units have been sold? How many have been taken back?

2. What is the reputation of the franchiser? This can be obtained from the Better Business Bureau and by personally contacting and meeting with other franchisees.

3. Have the figures the franchise company shows for an average perspective franchise been certified based upon existing performances of other franchises?

4. What kind of assistance will be provided to the franchisee? This includes the formal management training and continuing education seminars on upgrading management skills, promotion and financing assistance.

5. What assistance will the franchiser provide in seeking a possible location? What information is there to document why a certain site fits into the success profile of the franchiser?

6. How rigid is the company in allowing you, the franchisee, to make changes for your market, which might be different from other franchises?

One of the drawbacks of purchasing a franchise is that although you own the business you are subject to some very strict conveyance rules and regulations about how you actually operate the business. In the overall theory of franchising, this has many pluses, but for some individuals who are independent-minded and are looking to run the show, franchising might not be the most attractive means of going into business.

Patience is a virtue that carries a lot of wait.

6

THE WINNING BUSINESS PLAN

*The meeting of preparation with opportunity generates
the offspring called* luck.

ANTHONY ROBBINS

OVERVIEW

A "WINNING" BUSINESS PLAN MEANS THE DIFFERENCE BETWEEN AN accepted financing application and rejection. In this chapter, we'll uncover the secrets that turn a business plan into a "winner."

LOVE IT OR HATE IT, YOU NEED IT

> **Secret:** Investors and bankers are trained to make decisions based upon written—not verbal—reports.

The business plan causes a love-it or hate-it reaction in most small business owners. For those who are preparing a business plan for the first time, it is an exercise that is unfamiliar, tedious and foreign to their natural skills and what they do on a daily basis. It can be a process looked upon with great hesitation.

On the other hand, there are those who look upon the business plan for what it is: a tremendous marketing tool to communicate to bankers, investors and others.

The business plan should be thought of as a bridge to the land of capital. Without the business plan, there is no way to cross over the challenges and obstacles between you and your business dreams.

Professional managers, entrepreneurs and lenders are trained to analyze businesses by reviewing business plans. Verbal requests are forbidden. Investors prefer the written business plan because they want the supporting data that they need to make their decision in front of them in black-and-white.

That doesn't mean you can't use the business plan to tell the world what is so great about your business. In fact, you can even brag about yourself by writing in the third person what would be offensive if you were using the word "I".

For example, if you were to say, "I was able to reduce the overhead by 10 percent and I was also able to increase sales by 15 percent," it would sound pretty arrogant. The same information presented in the third person seems much more impressive: "Overhead was reduced by 10 percent and sales increased by 15 percent through the efforts of John Jones. A new cost savings program that shares part of the savings with the employees has been the key to these improvements in the company."

DO IT YOURSELF

Secret: New business plan software has taken the "brain damage" out of preparing a professional looking business plan in a relatively short period of time.

As a former banker, I'm a strong advocate of the owner or owners being involved in the preparation of the business plan. Hiring a ghostwriter who specializes in business plans is a waste of thousands of dollars and is a sure way of turning off investors and lenders.

The business plans prepared by professionals are beautiful documents to look at and read, no question. Unfortunately, they're usually written from the perspective of someone who has no financial risk at stake — and in most cases, no experience in your particular industry — trying to sell the investor or lender on an idea. If you aren't involved in the preparation of the plan, you could find yourself in the very embarrassing position of not being able to answer questions from the banker or investor about items the writer included in the plan to make the company look like something it's not.

The good news is that inexpensive user-friendly software greatly facilitates the process of preparing a business plan. Two excellent programs — Bizplan Builder and Tim Berry's Business Plan Tool Kit — are question-driven and have templates for projecting profit and loss and cash flow statements. These templates contain the formulas and perform the mathematical calculations; all you do is plug in your projected numbers. It's that simple and takes the "brain damage" out of preparing a business plan in a relatively short period of time.

Plan on the worst, hope for the best.

RULES FOR WINNING BUSINESS PLANS

There are certain rules that should be followed in preparing a business plan.

1. **The initial appearance of the business plan is very important.**
   It should be typed on a typewriter or printed on a laser printer on white paper. Wrinkles, smudge marks and stains on any

of the pages will reflect negatively on the business plan and your business.

2. **The business plan should be well written and grammatically correct.** You don't have to be an English major to write the business plan, just have someone skilled in sentence structure review the plan for you. Even a local high school, college, or graduate student or teacher can do this very reasonably.

3. **Be realistic and positive in tone.** It is important not to lie or mislead the reader by using false data or false projections. Don't be afraid to discuss some of the negative aspects that you, the business owner, are facing. But do use the business plan as a sales tool by showing your contingency plans to deal with any adverse situations.

4. **The business plan should be written at the level of the reader.** It is a major mistake to load the business plan with reams of technical jargon that distracts the reader's attention. The reader is not so much interested in the technical specs of your product as in the problems that will be solved by the product. Don't tell investors how to make a watch. Tell them how the watch is going to make their lives better by giving them the time of day.

5. **Don't write a thesis, just a business plan.** Another mistake is to oversell the company with a business plan that runs 40 to 60 pages. Can you imagine the first impression a lender or investor would have if you handed him or her a business plan that looked like a telephone directory of a small town? For most non-technical types of businesses, a good business plan can be written in 10 to 20 pages.

WHAT THE WINNING BUSINESS PLAN NEEDS

The following items should always be contained in the business plan to make it effective.

1. **A separate cover letter.** This letter should be personally addressed to the recipient, by name, title, company (if any), address and current date. Putting the date on the business plan itself can be looked upon negatively if it isn't current. The reader wants to feel that the information is right off the press, not shopped around for a couple of months before it got to his or her desk.

   The cover letter should also incorporate a summary of the loan request (see Chapter 3 for various types of loans and other details). A one-page loan proposal can be a very effective tool in giving you the upper hand in negotiations with your banker or investor. It allows the reader to quickly review the overall request and help set the stage for how thoroughly they will need to read the business plan. A loan request for $2 million will be read with greater scrutiny than a request for $50,000.

   Although it may be uncomfortable to prepare a loan proposal, you must understand that you are giving the key elements that the investor or lender needs up front to make the lending decision.

   Some of the items that should be included in a loan proposal are:

   a. **The important date the funds are needed. It's helpful and impressive if you can give as much lead time as possible — weeks, preferably months — before you need the**

funds. This gives a positive impression of your managerial skills and planning.

    b. The sort of entity that will be receiving the funds. Is the
loan going to a corporation, partnership, or sole propri-
etorship? It is also helpful to add in this section that the
owner or owners will also be guaranteeing the loan
request. This demonstrates to the lender the borrower's
confidence and willingness to stand behind the company
in the request for these funds.

    c. The amount of the loan request and the terms of repay-
ment. You should refer to a specific type of loan, whether
it be short-term or long-term.

    d. All collateral that is being offered. This should include
not only the collateral of the company in the form of
accounts receivable, inventory and equipment, but also
any personal assets, such as real estate, stocks and bonds,
you are willing to pledge in order to secure the loan. Do
not be overly generous in offering personal assets unless
the loan is weak and needs additional support. Let the
lender or investor make that decision.

2. **Table of Contents.** This is especially important to the reader
under tremendous time constraints or who is interested in a
particular section of the business plan. It allows the reader go
directly to that section, and it presents the business plan as
being well organized.

3. **Executive Summary.** This is usually a one- to two-page summary presented at the beginning of the business plan, but written at the very end of preparing the business plan itself. It con-
tains highlights that will allow the reader to get a feel for the

key elements covered in the remaining pages of the business plan.

4. **Concept.** This should be very brief and tightly focused to address how the proposed business's products or services will save customers and clients time, money, energy and make their lives better and happier. What problems will it solve? How will it reduce the stress in people's lives?

   Some of the key elements that should be covered in the concept are:

   a. **Who is the target market for the product or service of the business?**

   b. **What aspects of the product or service make it different from the competition?**

   c. **Are there patents filed or pending?**

   d. **What feature does your product or service have that the competition doesn't have?** Match those features with the benefits provided and the problems that would be solved.

5. **Company management and history.** For start-ups there will be no history to discuss in this section, but it will allow you to emphasize the background skills that management is bringing to the company. Emphasis should be placed upon previous successes in solving problems and turning around problem situations. A good example is if you were able to turn around your previous employer's manufacturing area in reducing costs by 10 percent and increasing productivity by 15 percent. Those are measurable accomplishments of turnaround situations that investors and lenders are looking for.

   This section should also cover the personnel in management

responsible for the three key areas: finance, marketing and human resources. Unfortunately in a start-up company or very small business, the owner is saddled with all three responsibilities. It is imperative to demonstrate how you will be able to obtain help in those areas. Do you have an accountant, a human resource specialist, or a marketing expert you can call upon to obtain the necessary information and help for your business?

Another idea that is popular and cost-effective is to have an advisory board made up of key people that complement the strengths of management. In exchange for the cost of a lunch, you are able to tap into the experience of experts in finance, marketing, human resources and computers.

6. **Description of the product or service.** This is probably one of the more challenging sections of the business plan to write, since the business owner seems to get carried away with how great the product or service is and goes into unnecessary detail. Lenders and investors want to know more about what makes this product or service sought after by the customer or client, and what makes it better than existing products or services on the market.

Secret: This is one section that most entrepreneurs want to leave out of the business plan. Why? They feel that the investor/banker will be "turned off" when they see in your business plan that you will be competing with the "Big Names," i.e., WalMart, Pizza Hut, IBM, etc. Don't make the fatal mistake of leaving the competition out of your business plan.

7. **Competition.** This section of the business plan allows the reader to gain confidence in your knowledge of the market and how well you have researched and checked out the competition and the potential for change.

But this is probably the section that most business owners hesitate including, because they lack the confidence of listing the names of their competitors, especially if the names are very familiar to the lender or investor. They are afraid the reader will ask, "Why would you be trying to compete with Wal-Mart or Kmart?"

However, to skip over this section in a business plan would be a major mistake. Lenders and investors realize that there is competition out there. They want to know what you're going to do differently that will make you unique and perceived as being more desirable by the marketplace. They also want to know if you're aware of the strengths and weaknesses of the competition.

This is an area where you can really make a company or idea stand out. It's a chance to turn lemons into lemonade. This is done very easily by constructing a grid at the beginning of the competition section. Set up the grid by putting the names of all of the competitors with your name at the top of the list on the left hand side of the grid. On the top horizontal section of the grid list some of the key features the marketplace is seeking: for example, 24-hour technical assistance, extended warranty options, user-friendly instructions, cost, financing, the availability of different models. This grid, when all the important features are graphically checked off, will make your company stand out from the competition as possessing most, if not all, of the qualities preferred by the marketplace.

COMPETITIVE EVALUATION AND CUSTOMER BENEFITS

	IN HOUSE ROASTING	FAST FRIENDLY SERVICE	COMPETITIVE PRICING	QUALITY PRODUCTS	CATERING TO BOTH COMMUTERS & SIT DOWN CUSTOMERS	INVITING AMBIANCE	CONVENIENT ACCESS	KNOWLEDGEABLE STAFF	CLEAN	GOURMET GIFT PACKAGES
THE BEAN COUNTER & ESPRESSO BAR	●	●	●	●	●	●	●	●	●	●
COFFEE CAFE	●		●	●					●	●
DRIVE UP JAVA					●	●				
KING TOP BREW			●				●			
CUP OF ART		●		●		●		●		
ESPRESSO EXPRESS			●							
COFFEE WAVE						●	●			

8. **Marketing plan.** Here is where you must document the benefits your customer gets from buying your product or service. It is important to be able to give statistics and cite studies that demonstrate the size of the market and any potential markets that can be looked upon for future expansion. In this section it must be made very clear why the market would want your product or service compared to others provided by your competitors.

Some of the items that need to be covered in the marketing plan are:

   a. **A crystal clear description of the potential market. The demographics must support and be described in terms of a typical customer or client, such age, sex, education, income level, geographical location and any other factors that would help segment the market. Marketing to a tar-**

get or niche is crucial in the success of any business venture, since very few products or services have universal appeal to all people.

b. Advantages and benefits of your products. Compare the cost of your competitor's product, the quality, the user-friendliness, and how users of your product will be able to save time or money, or in some cases both. You should also include testimonials of people who have used your product or service about the benefits that can further enhance the image of your product or service.

c. Size of the market and its potential. This is where you will want to use data obtained from the library or local college as source documentation that lends credibility to the size of the marketplace. Also document what motivates the customer or clients through the use of outside resources and studies. It is helpful to refer to a particular report that supports your ideas and include the full report in the Appendix. This is also a good area to cite experts who project future trends and how these trends show that your market is growing and is expected to continue growing.

d. Plan of attack. The investor or lender is very interested in the method you are going to use to sell your product and advertise to the ultimate target market you described earlier. The reader is looking for a detailed description of the process, for example, of going from manufacturing and distribution to the ultimate sales market. The type and medium of advertising and promotion to be used to reach the target market will be scrutinized closely to make sure that the business owner is using the rifle approach, rather than a shotgun approach. For example,

if you have described the target market as 35-50 years old, female, college educated, with one or two children, living in the suburbs, the investor or lender would probably question your advertising pro-gram if you're placing ads in such magazines as Guns and Ammo.

Secret: Be careful here! Don't yield to the easy temptation of overstating income and understating expenses in order to make your projections "look good."

---

9. **Financial data.** This includes the previous year's financial statements, if available, or for start-ups, projections. The financial projections should include a projected balance sheet for the next two years and profit and loss and cash flow statements for the next two years.

The first year needs to be done month by month to show any seasonal or other changes that the company anticipates. The second year can be done on a quarterly basis, since the lender and investor will have less confidence in what will happen in Year 2 and beyond.

For an existing business, the projections will be used in conjunction with the previous year's performance to create a credible forecast.

It has often been said that lenders and investors have never been presented with bad projections. All projections are looked upon as being optimistic, aggressive, and in some cases, unrealistic. There are several ways to overcome this built-in cynicism and prejudice. You can use the Robert Morris Association ratio analysis which gives key percentages and ratios for different business classifications. This is the textbook used by bankers and lenders in their own analysis; it is looked upon favorably if these numbers have already been incorporated into your projections. You can find the Robert Morris Association ratios at your local library.

Since the investors and lenders are looking at projections with a skeptical eye, the small business owner should prepare two sets of projections: one based upon what you hope the company will do with regards to sales and profits, and a second that is more tempered and conservative. If you provide only one set of projections, there is a possibility the reader will discount the figures so greatly it would make the numbers unacceptable for granting the loan. With two sets of projections, the reader will come up with a compromise between the two that will be the real figures used in the final analysis.

A very important aspect of projections is the key assumptions upon which you are basing your numbers: for example, sales, cost of goods sold, salaries, overhead. The assumptions need to provide details on how you're figuring on a 30 percent increase in sales for Year 2, or why salaries have gone down 12 percent when sales have increased 20 percent.

10. **Appendix.** The last section of the business plan should be put under a separate cover and not included with the plan itself. The Appendix is an area where you will include the resumes of the owner and key management people. The resumes should have such information as employment background, education, experience, skills, any special awards and areas of expertise.

If the business is established, a brief history should be included to give the reader an idea of how and when the business started, and any major changes that have taken place in the direction or operation of the business since its inception and why those changes were necessary.

You will also include in the Appendix studies and articles written about the industry supporting some of the conclusions in the marketing plan. You will also want to include collateral information about the technical aspects of the product, along with pictures and diagrams.

The Appendix can be very bulky. It is really supplementary reading to the main ideas contained in the business plan, which is why it should be under separate cover.

GET FEEDBACK ON YOUR PLAN

It is strongly advised after you have completed the business plan package that you submit it to several professionals with experience in reading and analyzing business plans. Listen to what they have to say and be prepared to make changes if they have suggestions to strengthen your presentation.

You can also get advice, for free, through the Small Business Development Corporation Center. See the Resource Guide in the back of this book for the location of the SBDC office nearest you, or call 703-448-6124.

Every day something is done that couldn't be done.

Often people attempt to live their lives backwards; they try to have more things, or more money, in order to do more of what they want so that they will be happier. The way it actually works is the reverse. You must be who you really are, then, do what you need to do, in order to have what you want.

MARGARET YOUNG

FINANCIAL
RESOURCE GUIDE

FINANCIAL RESOURCE GUIDE

ALABAMA

Statewide Financing Information and Resources: www.state.al.us

Alabama Development Office   (800) 248-0033
401 Adams Ave., Montgomery, AL 36130-4106

Economic Development
- Alabama Small Business Development   (205) 934-7260

Financial Assistance
- Economic Development Administration   (334) 223-7008
- Rural Development Administration   (334) 242-0400
- The TVA Economic Loan Fund   (800) 248-0033
- Revolving Loan Fund   (334) 652-3665

Minority/Women
- Office of Minority Business Enterprise   (334) 242-2220
- Appalachian Regional Grants   (334) 242-0400

Business Council of Alabama   (334) 834-6000
2 North Jackson Street, P.O. Box 76, Montgomery, AL 36101

SBA District Office   (205) 731-1344
2121 Eighth Ave, North, Suite 200, Birmingham, AL 35203-2398

Alabama Small Business Development Centers
University of Alabama at Birmingham   (205) 934-7260
1717 11th Ave., South, Suite 419, Birmingham, AL 35294
Auburn   (334) 844-4220   Mobile   (334) 460-6004

113

Birmingham (U. of AL.)	(205) 934-7260	Montgomery	(334) 229-4138
Florence	(205) 760-4624	Troy	(334) 670-3771
Huntsville	(205) 535-2061	Tuscaloosa	(205) 348-7011
Jacksonville	(205) 782-5271	(U. of AL)	
Livingston	(334) 652-3665		

Alabama Small Business Investment Companies

Birmingham-Alabama Small Business Investment Co.	(205) 324-5231
Birmingham-Javelin Capital (205) 943-6662	
Huntsville-Hickory Venture Capital Corporation	(205) 539-1931
Huntsville-FJC Growth Capital Corporation	(205) 922-2918
Mobile-Alabama Capital Corporation	(334) 476-0700
Mobile-First SBIC Alabama	(334) 476-0700

Alabama Certified Development Companies

Birmingham-Birmingham Citywide Local Devel. Corp.	(205) 254-2799
Mobile-Greater Mobile Development Corporation	(334) 434-7591
Montgomery-Southern Development Council	(334) 244-1801
Mountain Brook-Alabama Community Development Corp.	(205) 870-3360

Micro Loans

Wetumpka-Elmore Community Action	(334) 567-4361

ALASKA

Statewide Financing Information and Resources: **www.state.ak.us**

Department of Commerce and Economic Development   **(907) 465-2510**
State Office Building, Ninth Floor   (800) 478-LOAN
333 Willoughby Ave., P.O. Box 110800
Juneau, AK 99811-0800

Economic Development
- Division of Trade and Development
  Business Development Information Network   (907) 465-3961
- Economic Development, Fairbanks
  Native Association, Inc.   (907) 452-1648

Financial Assistance
- Division of Trade and Development   (907) 465-2017
- Division of Investments   (907) 465-2510
  Commercial Fishing Loan Program
  Small Business Economics Development Revolving Loan Fund
- Alaska Industrial Development   (907) 269-3000

Loan Participation Program
Development Finance Program
• Small Business Economic Development
  Revolving Loan Fund   (800) 478-LOAN

Minority/Women
• Alaska Business Development Center   (800) 478-3474
• Minority Business Development Center   (907) 274-5400

Rural Development
• Division of Community and Rural Development
  Rural Development Assistance ·   (907) 465-5539

Alaska State Chamber of Commerce   (907) 586-2323
217 Second Street, Suite 201, Juneau, AK 99801

SBA District Office   (907) 271-4022
222 W. Eighth Ave., Rm. A-36, P.O. Box 67, Ankorage, AK 99513-7559

Alaska Small Business Development Centers
University of Alaska at Anchorage   (907) 274-7232
430 West Seventh Avenue, Suite 110, Anchorage, AK 99501
Fairbanks   (907) 474-6400   Kenai   (907) 283-3335
Fairbanks   (907) 456-1701   Wasilla   (907) 373-7232
Juneau   (907) 463-3789

Micro Loans
Juneau-Southeast Alaska Small Business Development Center (907) 463-3789

ARIZONA

Statewide Financing Information and Resources: www.state.az.us

Business Development Finance Corporation   (520) 722-5626
186 East Broadway Boulevard, Tucson, AX 85701

Economic Development
• Arizona Department of Commerce   (520) 628-6850
• Arizona Small Business Development Center Network (602) 731-8720
• Arizona Business Connection   (520) 628-6690
• Commerce and Economic Development Commission   (602) 280-1341
• Business Hotline   (520) 791-2519

Financial Assistance
- Business Development Finance Corporation	(800) 264-3377
- Small Business Financing Programs	(602) 280-1341
- Minority - Women	(800) 542-5684

Arizona Chamber of Commerce	(602) 248-9172
1221 East Osborn Road, Suite 100, Phoenix, AZ 85014

SBA District Office
2828 North Central Avenue, Suite 800, Phoenix, AZ 85004-1093

Arizona SBDC Network	(602) 731-8720
2411 West 14th Street, Room 132, Tempe, AZ 85281

Coolidge	(520) 426-4341	Prescott	(520) 757-0894
Flagstaff	(520) 526-5072	Show Low	(800) 266-7232
Holbrook	(520) 537-2976	Kingman	(520) 757-0894
Sierra Vista	(520) 515-5478	Nogales	(520) 287-2569
Thatcher	(520) 428-8590	Payson	(520) 474-8821
Tucson	(520) 748-4906	Phoenix	(602) 392-5223
Yuma	(520) 341-1650		

Arizona Small Business Investment Companies
Phoenix - Sundance Venture Partners, LP	(602) 252-5373
Tucson - First Commerce & Loan, LP	(602) 298-2500

Arizona Certified Development Companies
Phoenix - Southwest Business Finance Corporation	(602) 495-6495
Tucson - Business Development Finance Corporation	(602) 623-3377

Micro Loans
Phoenix - Chicanos Por La Causa	(602) 257-0700
Tucson - PPEP Housing Development	(602) 622-3553
(Greater Maricopa County)

ARKANSAS

Statewide Financing Information and Resources:	www.state.ar.us

Arkansas Industrial Development Commission	**(501) 682-1121**
One State Capitol Mall, Little Rock, AR 72201

Economic Development
- Advocacy	(501) 682-7325

- Corporate Extension Service   (501) 671-2000
- The Arkansas Science and Technology Authority   (501) 324-9006
- General Business Assistance (SCORE)   (501) 324-5893
- Genesis Technology Business Incubator   (501) 575-7227
- Industrial Development   (501) 682-7675
- Small Business Programs   (501) 682-7782

Financial Assistance
- Arkansas Capital Corporation   (501) 374-9247
- Bond Guaranty Program   (501) 682-7682

Minority/Women
- Minority Business Development Program   (501) 682-1060

Arkansas State Chamber of Commerce   (501) 374-9225
410 Cross Street, P.O. Box 3645, Little Rock, AR 77203

SBA District   (501) 324-5871
2120 Riverfront Dr., Suite 100, Little Rock, AR 72202-1747

Arkansas Small Business Development Centers
University of Arkansas at Little Rock   (501) 324-9043
100 South Main Street, Suite 401, Little Rock, AR 72201

Arkadelphia	(501) 230-5224	West Memphis	(501) 733-6767
Fayetteville	(501) 575-5148	Magnolia	(501) 234-4030
Fort Smith	(501) 785-1376	Pine Bluff	(501) 536-0654
Harrison	(501) 741-8009	St. University	(501) 972-3517
Hot Springs	(501) 624-5448	Stuttgart	(501) 673-8707

Arkansas Small Business Investment Company
Little Rock-Small Business Investment Capital, Inc.   (501) 455-6599

Arkansas Certified Development Companies
Batsville-White River Planning & Development District, Inc.   (501) 793-5233
Fort Smith-Western Arkansas Planning & Devel. District, Inc.   (501) 785-2651
Harrison-Northwest Arkansas Development Company   (501) 741-8009
Hot Springs-W. Central Ark. Planning & Devel. District, Inc.   (501) 624-1036
Jonesboro-East Arkansas Planning & Development District   (501) 932-3957
Little Rock-Arkansas Certified Development Corporation   (501) 374-9247
Magnolia-Southwest Arkansas Regional Development Corp.   (501) 234-4039

Micro Loans
Arkadelphia-Arkansas Enterprises Group   (501) 246-9739

Forest City-Delta Community Development   (501) 633-9113
Batesville-White River Development   (501) 793-5233

CALIFORNIA

Statewide Financing Information and Resources: www.state.ca.us

California Office of Small Business   **(916) 324-1295**
California Trade and Commerce Agency
801 K Street, Suite 1700, Sacramento, CA 95814

Economic Development
* Small Business Development Center   (916) 324-5068
* Office of Business Development   (916) 322-3520
* Office of Economic Research   (916) 324-5853
* Office of Small Business   (916) 324-1295
* Small Business Helpline   (916) 327-4257

Financial Assistance
* Small Business Loan Guarantee Program   (916) 324-1295

International Trade
* California Office of Export Finance   (714) 562-5519

Minority/Women
* Office of Small and Minority Business   (916) 322-5060

California Chamber of Commerce   (916) 444-6670
1201 K Street, 12th Floor, P.O. Box 1736, Sacramento, CA 95812-1736

SBA District Offices - Fresno   (209)-487-5789
2719 North Air Fresno Drive, Suite 107, Fresno, CA 93727-1547
Glendale   (818) 552-3210
   330 North Brand Blvd., Suite 1200, Glendale, CA 91203-2304
Sacramento   (916) 498-6410
   660 J Street, Suite 215, Sacramento, CA 95814-2413
Santa Ana   (714) 550-5440
   200 West Santa Ana Blvd., Suite 700, Santa Ana, CA 92701
San Diego   (619) 557-5440
   550 West C Street, Suite 550, San Diego, CA 92101
San Francisco   (415) 744-6820
   211 Main Street, Fourth Floor, San Francisco, CA 94105-1988

FINANCIAL RESOURCE GUIDE

California Small Business Development Centers

California Trade and Commerce Agency   (916) 324-5068
801 K Street, Suite 1700, Sacramento, CA 95814-3520

Aptos	(408) 479-6136	Napa	(707) 253-3210
Auburn	(916) 885-5488	Oakland	(510) 893-4114
Bakersfield	(805) 322-5881	Chico	(916) 895-9017
Palm Springs	(619) 864-1311	Chula Vista	(916) 482-6391
Clearlake	(707) 995-3440	Pomona	(909) 629-2247
Concord	(510) 646-5377	Crescent City	(707) 464-2168
Riverside	(909) 781-2345	El Centro	(619) 312-9800
Eureka	(707) 446-9720	Sacramento	(916) 563-3210
Fairfield	(707) 864-3382	Fresno	(209) 275-1223
Santa Ana	(714) 647-1172	Gilroy	(408) 847-0373
Santa Monica	(310) 398-8883	Irvine	(714) 509-2990
Santa Rosa	(707) 524-1770	La Jolla	(619) 453-9388
Stockton	(209) 474-5089	Los Angeles	(213) 846-1710
Torrance	(310) 787-6466	Markleville	(916) 694-2475
Merced	(209) 725-3800	Visalia	(209) 625-3051
Modesto	(209) 521-6177	San Francisco	(415) 561-1890

California Small Business Investment Companies

Alhambra-Calsafe Capital Corporation	(818) 289-3400
Beverly Hills-Ally Finance Corporation	(310) 550-8100
Cupertino-Novus Ventures, LP	(408) 252-3900
Cupertino-Sundance Venture Partners, LP	(408) 257-8100
Foundation Valley-First American Capital Funding, Inc.	(714) 965-7190
Fremont-Opportunity Capital Corporation	(510) 795-7000
Fremont-Opportunity Capital Partners II, L.P.	(510) 795-7000
Fresno-San Joaquin Investment Group, Inc.	(209) 233-3580
Glendale-Magna Pacific Investments	(818) 547-0809
Hayward-Asian American Capital Corporation	(510) 887-6888
Inglewood-Imperial Ventures, Inc.	(310) 417-5600
Laguna Hills-Hall Capital Management	(714) 707-5096
Los Altos-Aspen Venture West II, LP	(415) 917-5670
Los Altos-VI Capital, LP	(415) 949-9862
Los Angeles-Best Finance	(213) 937-1636
Los Angeles-Charterway Investment Corporation	(213) 689-9107
Los Angels-Union Venture Corporation	(213) 236-4092
Newport Beach-Marwit Capital Corporation	(714) 640-6234
Redwood City-Draper Fisher Associates, LP	(415) 599-9000
San Diego-Sorrento Growth Partners I, LP	(619) 452-3100
San Francisco-Bentley Capital	(415) 362-2868
San Francisco-Jupiter Partners	(415) 421-9990

San Francisco-Positive Enterprises, Inc.	(415) 885-6600
San Francisco-VK Capital Company	(415) 391-5600
Sherman Oaks-Western General Capital Corporation	(818) 986-5038

California Certified Development Companies

Arcata-Arcata Economic Development Corporation	(707) 822-4616
Arvin-Arvin Development Corporation	(805) 861-2041
Bakersfield-Mid State Development Corporation	(805) 322-4241
Citrus Heights-Econ. Devel. Foundation of Sacramento, Inc.	(916) 962-3669
Davis-California Statewide Certified Development	(916) 756-9310
Fresno-Fresno Certified Development Corporation	(209) 485-5735
Jackson-Amador Economic Development Corporation	(209) 223-0351
La Habra-La Habra Local Development Company, Inc.	(310) 690-6400
Lompoc-Central Coast Development Corporation	(805) 736-1445
Long Beach-Long Beach Area Certified Development Corp.	(310) 983-7450
Modesto-Stanislaus County Economic development Corp.	(209) 521-9333
Monterey Park-Business Finance Center	(213) 890-7049
Ontario-Enterprise Funding Corporation	(909) 981-2744
Pittsburgh-Los Medanos Fund, A Local Devel. Company	(510) 439-1056
Redding-\economic Development Corp. of Shasta County	(916) 225-5300
Sacramento-Greater Sacramento Certified Devel. Corp.	(916) 339-1096
San Diego-CD Small Business Finance Corporation	(619) 291-3594
San Francisco-Bay Area Business Development Company	(415) 541-0694
Santa Ana-Santa Ana Economic Development Corporation	(714) 647-1143
Stockton-Tracy/San Joaquin County CDC	(209) 468-2266
Tulare-Tulare County Economic Development Corporation	(209) 688-6666
Walnut Creek-Bay Area Employment Development	(510) 926-1020

COLORADO

Statewide Financing Information and Resources:	**www.state.co.us**

Office of Business Development   **(303) 892-3840**
1625 Broadway, Suite 1710, Denver, CO 80202

Economic Development
• Office of Business Development	(303) 892-3840
• Colorado FIRST Customized Training Program	(303) 892-3840
• Business Assistance	(303) 592-5920

Financial Assistance
• Colorado Housing And Fiance Authority	(303) 297-2432
• Office of Business Development Finance Division	(303) 892-3840

Minority/Women
- Minority Business Office   (303) 892-3840
- Women's Business Office   (303) 892-3840
- MiCasa Resource Center   (303) 573-1302

Colorado Association of Commerce & Industry   (303) 831-7411
1776 Lincoln Street, Suite 1200, Denver, CO 80203

SBA District Office   (303) 844-3984
721 19th Street, Suite 426, Denver, CO80202-2599

Colorado Small Business Development Centers
Office of Business Development   (303) 892-3809
Colorado Small Business Development Center
1625 Broadway, Suite 1710, Denver, CO 80202

Alamosa	(719) 589-7372		
Glenwood Springs	(800) 621-1647	Aurora	(303) 341-4849
Grand Junction	(970) 243-5242	Boulder	(303) 442-1475
Greeley (CoC)	(970) 352-3661		
Colorado Springs	(719) 592-1894	Lakewood	(303) 987-0710
Craig	(970) 824-7078	Lamar	(719) 336-8141
Delta	(970) 874-8772		
Littleton (CoC)	(303) 795-0142	Denver (CC)	(303) 620-8076
Pueblo	(719) 549-3224	Durango	(970) 247-7009
Stratton	(719) 348-5596	Fort Collins	(970) 226-0881
Trinidad	(719) 846-5645	Fort Morgan	(970) 267-3351
Westminster	(303) 460-1032		

Colorado Small Business Investment Company
Denver-Hanifen Imhoff Mezzanine Fund, LP   (303) 291-5209

Colorado Certified Development Companies
Denver-Denver Urban Economic Development Corporation (303) 296-5570
Denver-Small Business Finance Corporation   (303) 893-8989
Denver-Front Range Regional Economic Development   (303) 657-0010
Colorado Spring-Pikes Peak Regional
Development Corporation   (719) 471-2044
Pueblo-CEDD Development Company   (719) 545-8680

Micro Loans
Denver-Denver Capital Corp.   (303) 534-6161
Denver-Greater Denver Local Development Corp.   (303) 860-0242

CONNECTICUT

Statewide Financing Information and Resources:	**www.state.ct.us**

Office of Small Business Services   **(860) 258-4200**
Department of Economic and Community Development
865 Brook Street, Rocky Hill, CT 06067-34056

Economic Development
- One-Stop Business Registry   (800) 392-2122
- Connecticut Innovations   (800) 392-2122
  -R&D, technology transfer, manufacturing applications
- Office of Business Ombudsman   (860) 258-4200
- Connecticut State Technology Extension Program   (800) 392-2122

Financial Assistance
- Connecticut Development Authority   (800) 392-2122
- Manufacturing Assistance   (800) 392-2122
  -tax credits, loan guarantees, investment and direct loans
- Connecticut Works Fund   (800) 392-2122
- Connecticut Works Funds   (800) 392-2122
  -loan guarantees, direct loans
- Connecticut Innovations, Inc.   (800) 392-2122
  -early state financing for high-tech companies

Minority/Women
- Urban lending   (800) 392-2122
  -targeted to women and minorities in distressed cities

Connecticut Business & Industry Association   (860) 244-1900
370 Asylum Street, Hartford, CT 06103

SBA District Office   (860) 240-4700
330 Main Street, Second Floor, Hartford, CT 06106

Connecticut Small Business Development Centers
University of Connecticut   (860) 486-4135
School of Business Admin., 2 Bourn Place, U-94, Storrs. CT 06269-5094

Bridgeport	(203) 330-4813	Groton	(860) 405-9002
Danbury	(203) 743-5565	Middletown	(203) 344-2158
Danielson	(203) 774-1133	New Haven	(203) 782-4390
Stamford	(203) 359-3220 x 302		
Willimantic	(860) 465-5349	Waterbury	(203) 757-8937
W. Hartford	(860) 570-9109		

Connecticut Small Business Investment Companies

Cheshire - AB SBIC, Inc.	(203) 272-0203
Farmington - Capitol Resource Company	(860) 677-1113
New Canaan - RFE Capital Partners, LP	(203) 966-2800
New Canaan - RFE Investment Partners V, LP	(203) 966-2800
New Haven - All State Venture Capital Corporation	(203) 787-5028
Hartford - First New England Capital, LP	(860) 293-3333
Rowayton - Canaan SBIC, LP	(203) 855-0400
Stamford - TSG Ventures, Inc.	(203) 406-1500
West Hartford - Capital Resource Co, of Connecticut	(203) 236-4336
Westport - Marcon Capital Corp.	(203) 221-8402

Connecticut Certified Development Companies

Danbury - Housatonic Industrial Development Corporation	(203) 743-0306
Hartford - Greater Hartford Business Development Center, Inc.	(860) 527-1301
Rocky Hill - Connecticut Business Development Corporation	(860) 258-7855

Micro Loans

New Haven - New Haven Community Investment Corp.	(203) 776-6172

DELAWARE

Statewide Financing Information and Resources:	**www.state.de.us**
Delaware Economic Development Office	**(302) 739-4271**
99 Kings Highway, P.O. Box 1401, Dover, DE 19902	

Economic Development/Procurement Assistance

• Business Development	(302) 739-4271
• Business Research	(302) 739-4221
• Education, Training and Recruitment	(302) 739-4271
• Small Business Advocate	(302) 739-4271

Financial Assistance

• Business Finance	(302) 739-4271
• Delaware Economic Development Authority	(302) 739-4271

Delaware State Chamber of Commerce	(302) 655-7221
1201 North Orange St., Suite 200, P.O. Box 671, Wilmington, DE 19899	

SBA Branch Office	(302) 573-6294
824 North Market Street, Suite 610, Wilmington, DE 19801-3011	

Delaware Small Business Development Centers
University of Delaware   (302) 831-1555
-Purnell Hall, Suite 005, Newark, DE 19716-2711
Dover   (302) 678-1555   Georgetown   (302) 856-1555

Delaware Small Investment Companies
Wilmington - Blue Rock Capital   (302) 426-0981
Wilmington - PNC Capital   (303) 427-5895

Delaware Certified Development Companies
Dover - Delaware Development Corporation   (302) 739-4271
Wilmington - Wilmington Economic Development Corp.   (302) 571-9088

Micro Loans
Wilmington - Wilmington Economic Development   (302) 571-9088

DISTRICT OF COLUMBIA

Statewide Financing Information and Resources: www.state.dc.us

Office of Economic Development   **(202) 727-6600**
717 14th Street, NW, Twelfth Floor, Washington, DC 20005

Economic Development
• Business Center   (202) 727-7100
• Department of Consumer and Regulatory Affairs   (202) 727-7000
• Incorporation/Corporate Division   (202) 727-7278

Financial Assistance
• Economic Development Finance Corporation   (202) 775-8815
• Industrial Revenue Bond Program   (202) 727-6600
• Loan Guarantee Program   (202) 535-1942

Minority Women
• Department of Human Rights and Minority
  Business Development   (302) 724-1385
• Washington, D.C. Minority Business
  Development Center   (202) 785-2886

District of Columbia Chamber of Commerce   (202) 638-3222

SBA District Office   (202) 606-4000
110 Vermont Avenue, NW, Suite 900, Washington, DC 20043-4500

District of Columbia Small Business Development Centers

Howard University	(202) 806-1550

Metropolitan Washington SBDC
2600 Sixth St., NW, Room 125, Washington, DC 20059

Development Corporation of Columbia Heights	(202) 483-4986
East of the River Community Development Corporation	(202) 561-4975
SBA Business Information Center	(202) 606-4000 x279
George Washington University Small Business Clinic	(202) 994-7463
Marshall Heights Community Development Organization	(202) 396-1200
Ward Five Community Development	(202) 396-1200
Washington District Office	(202) 606-4000

District of Columbia Small Business Investment Companies

Washington, DC - Allied Investment Corporation	(202) 331-1112
Washington, DC - Allied Investment Corporation	(202) 331-1112
Washington, DC - Broadcast Investment Corp.	(202) 496-9250
Washington, DC - Capital Health Partners	(202) 965-2338

District of Columbia Certified Development Company

Washington, DC - Community First, Inc.	(202) 338-8993

Micro Loans

Washington, DC - Arch Development Corp.	(202) 889-5023
Washington, DC - J Street Development	(202) 544-8353

FLORIDA

Statewide Financing Information and Resources:	**www.state.fl.us**

Enterprise Florida	**(305) 377-8766**

Suntrust Center
200 So. Orange Ave., Suite 1200, Orlando, FL 32801

Economic Development

• Technology Division	(407) 425-5313
• Tourism, Trade and Economic Development	(904) 487-2568
• Manufacturing Technology Division	(954) 941-0115

Financial Assistance

• Capital Division	(407) 425-5313
• Grant Division	(904) 488-6300

Minority/Women
- Enterprise Florida (305) 377-8766

Florida Chamber of Commerce (904) 425-1200
136 S. Bronough St., Tallahassee, FL 32302

SBA District Offices
Coral Gables (305) 536-5521
1320 So. Dixie Hwy., Suite 301, Coral Gables, FL 33146-29211
Jacksonville (904) 443-1900
7825 Baymeadows Way, Ste. 100, Jacksonville, FL 32256-7504

Florida Small Business Development Centers
University of West Florida (904) 444-2060
19 West Garden Street, Suite 300, Pensacola, FL 32501

Bartow	(941) 534-4370	Boca Raton	(561) 362-5620
Miami, FL	(305) 919-5790	Dania	(954) 987-0100
Daytona Beach	(904) 947-5463	Ocala	(352) 629-8051
Fort Lauderdale	(954) 771-6520	Orlando	(407) 823-5554
Fort Myers	(941) 590-7316		
Pensacola (U. of W. FL)	(904) 474-2908	Fort Pierce	(561) 462-4756
Pensacola (Tech)	(904) 444-2066		
Fort Walton Beach	(904) 863-6543	Sanford	(407) 328-4722
Gainesville (CDC)	(377) 377-5621	St. Petersburg	(813) 341-4456
Jacksonville	(904) 646-2476	Tallahassee	(904) 599-3407
Lynn Haven	(904) 271-1108	Tampa	(813) 974-4371
Melbourne	(407) 632-1111 x 33201		

Florida Small Business Investment Companies
Miami - BAC Investment Corporation (305) 693-5919
Tampa - Market Capital Corporation (813) 248-5781
N. Miami Beach - PMC Corporation (933) 933-5858

Florida Certified Development Companies
Gainesville - North Cent. Florida Areawide Devel. Co., Inc. (352) 955-2199
Jacksonville - Business Devel. Corp. of Northeast Florida, Inc. (904) 363-6350
Jacksonville - Jacksonville Economic Development Company (904) 630-1906
Lake Worth - Florida Business Development Corporation (561) 433-0233
St. Petersburg - St. Petersbury CDC, Inc. (813) 895-2504
Tallahassee - Florida First Capital Finance Corporation, Inc. (904) 487-0466
Tampa - Tampa Bay Economic Development Corporation (813) 242-5442

Micro Loans

Pensacola - Community Equity Investments	(904) 444-2234
Gainesville - United Gainesville Community Development	(904) 376-8891

GEORGIA

Statewide Financing Information and Resources:	**www.state.ga.us**

Georgia Department of Industry, Trade, and Tourism   **(404) 656-3545**
P.O. Box 1776, Atlanta, GA 30301

Economic Development
- Small Business Revitalization Program   (404) 656-3872
- Business Development Corporation of Georgia   (404) 656-3556

Financial Assistance
- Department of Industry, Trade and Tourism   (404) 656-3556
- Business Loan Program
  -Business and Industrial Loan Program
  -Business Loan Guarantee Program
  -Capital Network
  -Intermediary Relending Program
  -Regional Revolving Loan Funds

Minority/Women
- Office of Small and Minority Affairs   (404) 656-6315

Georgia Chamber of Commerce   (404) 223-2264
233 Peachtree St., Suite 200, Atlanta, GA 30303

SBA District Office   (404) 347-2441
1720 Peachtree Road, NW, Suite 600, Atlanta, GA 30309

Georgia Small Business Development Centers
University of Georgia   (706) 542-6762
Business Outreach Services
Chicopee Complex 1180 E. Broad St., Athens, GA 30602-5412

Albany	(912) 430-4303	Lawrenceville	(770) 806-2124
Athens (NE GA Dist.)	(706) 542-7436	Macon	(912) 751-6592
Athens (NW GA Dist.)	(770) 542-6756	Narietta	(770) 423-6450
Atlanta	(404) 651-3550	Morrow	(770) 961-3440
Augusta	(706) 737-1790	Savannah	(912) 356-2755
Brunswick	(912) 264-7343	Statesboro	(912) 681-5194

Columbus	(706) 649-7433	Valdosta	(912) 245-3738
Decatur	(404) 373-6930	Warner Robbins	(912) 953-9356
Gainesville	(770) 531-5681	Kennesaw	(770) 423-6450
LaGrange	(706) 812-7353		

Georgia Small Business Investment Companies
Atlanta-Cordova Capital Partners, LP-Enhanced Appreciation (770) 951-1542
Atlanta-Renaissance Capital Corporation (404) 658-9061
Atlanta-EGI/Nat West Ventures (770) 399-5633

Georgia Certified Development Companies
Americus-Middle Flint Area Development Corporation (912) 931-2909
Athens-Certified Development Company (706) 369-5650
Atlanta-Atlanta Local Development Company (404) 658-7000
Atlanta-Business Growth Corporation of Georgia (770) 434-0273
Atlanta-Economic Development Corp. of Fulton Co. (404) 730-8078
Augusta-CSRA Local Development Corporation (706) 737-1823
Brunswick-Coastal Area District Development Authority (912) 261-2500
Camilla-Sowega Economic Development Corporation (912) 336-5617
Columbus-Uptown Columbus, Inc. (706) 596-0111
Dalton-North Georgia Certified Development Company (706) 226-1110
Eastman-Heart of Georgia Area Development Corporation (912) 374-4773
Gainesville-Georgia Mountain Regional EDC (770) 536-7839
LaGrange-Troup County Local Development Corporation (706) 884-8671
Macon-Development Corporation of Middle Georgia (912) 751-6160
Savannah-Small Business Assistance Corp. of Savannah (912) 232-4700
Valdosta-South Georgia Regional Development Corporation (912) 333-5277
Waycross-Financial Services Corp. of Southeast Georgia (912) 285-6097

Micro Loans
Atlanta-Fulton County Development (404) 659-5955
Savannah-Small Business Assistance (912) 232-4700

HAWAII

Statewide Financing Information and Resources: **www.state.hi.us**

Department of Business, Economic Development and Tourism **(808) 586-2591**
250 South Hotel Street, 5th Floor, Honolulu, HI 96813

Economic Development
• Business Action Center   (808) 586-2545

- Pacific Business Center   (808) 956-6286
- Business Information and Counseling Center   (808) 522-8131

Financial Assistance
- Financial Assistance Branch   (808) 586-2576
- Agricultural Loan Division   (808) 973-9460

Minority/Women
- Women in Business Committee   (808) 541-3024

The Chamber of Commerce of Hawaii   (808) 545-4300
1132 Bishop Street, Suite 200, Honolulu, HI

SBA District Office   (808) 541-2990
300 Ala Moana Blvd., Room 2213, Honolulu, Hi 96850-4981

Hawaii Small Business Development Centers
Hilo (University of Hawaii at Hilo)   (808) 933-3515
200 West Kawili Street, Hilo, HI 96720-4091
Honolulu   (808) 522-8131   Lihue   (808) 246-1748
Kihel   (808) 875-2402

Small Business Investment Centers
Honolulu-Bancorp Hawaii   (808) 537-8613

Hawaii Certified Development Company
Honolulu-HEDCO Local Development Corporation   (808) 521-6502

Micro Lenders
Honolulu-The Immigrant Center   (808) 845-3918

IDAHO

Statewide Financing Information and Resources: www.state.id.us

Department of Commerce   **(208) 334-2470**
700 West State Street, P.O. Box 83720, Boise, ID 83720-2700

Economic Development
- Division of Economic Development   (208) 334-2470
- Idaho Business Network   (808) 334-2470

Financial Assistance
- Pan Handle Area Council
  Business Center for Innovation and Development   (208) 772-0584
- Idaho Innovation Center   (208) 523-1026

Minority/Women
- Associated General Contractors of America   (208) 344-2531

Idaho Association of Commerce & Industry   (208) 343-1849
802 West Bannock St., Suite 308, P.O. box 389, Boise, ID 83701

SBA District Office   (208) 334-1696
1020 Main Street, Suite 290, Boise, ID 83702-5745

Idaho Small Business Development Centers
Boise State University   (208) 385-1640
College of Business, 1910 University Drive, Boise, ID 83725

Boise	(208) 385-3875	Pocatello	(208) 232-4921
Idaho Falls	(208) 523-1087	Post Falls	(208) 769-3296
Lewiston	(208) 799-2465	Twin Falls	(208) 733-9554 x2450

Idaho Certified Development Companies
Boise-Capital Matrix, Inc.   (208) 322-7033
Hayden-Panhandle Area Council, Inc.   (208) 772-0584
Pocatello-Eastern Idaho Development Corporation   (208) 234-7541
Rexburg-East Central Idaho Planning & Development Co.   (208) 356-4525
Twin Falls-Region IV Development Corporation, Inc.   (208) 736-3064

Micro Loans
Hayden-Panhandle Area Council   (208) 772-0584

ILLINOIS

Statewide Financing Information and Resources: www.state.il.us

Small Business Development Center   **(217) 524-5856**
Department of commerce and Community Affairs
620 East Adams Street, Third Floor, Springfield, IL 62701

Economic Development
- Illinois First Stop Program-Toll-free in Illinois   (800) 252-2923
- Illinois Business Hotline-Toll-free in Illinois   (800) 252-2923
- Illinois SBDC Network-Toll-free in Illinois   (800) 252-2923

Financial Assistance
* Loan Administration Division-Springfield   (217) 782-3891
  Chicago   (312) 814-2308

Minority/Women
* Office of Minority Business Development   (312) 814-3540
* Office of Women's Business Development   (312) 814-7176

The Illinois State Chamber of Commerce   (312) 983-7100
311 South Wacker Drive, Suite 1500, Chicago, IL 60606-6619

SBA District Offices-Chicago   (312) 353-4528
500 West Madison St., room 1250, Chicago, IL 60661-2511
Springfield (Branch Office)   (217) 492-4416
511 West Capitol Avenue, Suite 302, Springfield, IL 62704

Illinois Small Business Development Centers
Department of Commerce & Community Affairs   (217) 524-5856
620 East Adams Street, 3rd Floor, Springfield, IL62701
Chicago
  Asian American Alliance   (312) 202-0600
  Back of the Yards Neighborhood Council   (312) 523-4419
  DCAA State of Illinois Center   (312) 814-6111
  18th Street Development Corporation   (312) 733-2287
  Greater N. Pulaski Economic Development Council   (312) 384-2262
  Industrial Council   (312) 421-3941
  Latin/American Chamber of Commerce   (312) 252-5211
  Midwest Chicago Business Association   (773) 826-4055
  North Business & Industrial Council   (312) 588-5855
  University at Illinois at Chicago   (773) 996-4057
  Women's Business Development   (312) 853-3477

Aurora	(630) 801-7900	Ina	(618) 437-5321 x335
Carbondale	(618) 536-2424	Joliet	(815) 727-6544
Centralia	(618) 532-2049	Kankakee	(815) 933-0376
Crystal Lake	(815) 455-6098	Macomb	(309) 298-2211
Danville	(217) 442-7232	Monmouth	(309) 734-4664
Decatur	(217) 875-8284	Oglesby	(815) 223-1740
Dixon	(815) 288-5605	Olney	(618) 395-3011
East Moline	(309) 755-2200	Palos Hills	(707) 974-5468
East St. Louis	(618) 583-2270	Peoria	(309) 677-2992
Edwardsville	(618) 692-2929	Quincy (Proc.)	(217) 228-5511
Elgin	(847) 888-7675		
River Grove	(708) 456-0300 x3593		

Evanston	(847) 866-1817	Rockford	(815) 968-4087
Glen Ellyn	(630) 942-2771	Springfield	(217) 789-1017
Godfrey	(618) 466-3411	Ullin	(618) 634-9618
Grayslake	(847) 223-3633	University Park	(708) 534-4929
Harrisburg	(618) 252-5001		

Illinois Small Business Investment Companies

Chicago-ABN AMRO Capital	(312) 904-6445
Chicago-Nesbitt Burns Equity	(312) 461-2021
Chicago-Shorebank Capital Corporation	(312) 371-7030

Illinois Certified Development Companies

Chicago-CANDO City-Wide Development Corporation	(312) 939-7171
Chicago-Greater North-Pulaski Local Development Corp.	(312) 384-7074
Chicago-Somercor 504, Inc.	(312) 360-3163
Collinsville-Small Business Finance Alliance	(618) 344-4080
Northbrook-Greater Metropolitan Chicago Development	(708) 251-2756
Peoria-Illinois Business Financial Servies	(815) 987-8127
Salem-South Central IL. Regional Planning & Devel. Comm.	(618) 548-4234
Springfield-Illinois Small Business Growth corporation	(217) 522-2772
University Park-South towns Business Growth Corporation	(708) 534-4924
Waukegan-Lake County Economic Development Corp.	(847) 360-6350

Micro Loans

| Chicago-Illinois Development Finance Authority | (312) 793-5586 |
| Peoria-Economic Dev. Council | (309) 676-7500 |

INDIANA

Statewide Financing Information and Resources: www.state.in.us

State Information Center   **(317) 233-0800**
402 West Washington Street, Room W160, Indianapolis, IN 46204

Economic Development
- Indiana Department of Commerce   (317) 232-8800
  Administrative Service Division   (317) 232-8782
  Business Development Division   (317) 232-8888
- Indiana Small Business Development Corp. (ISBD Corp.)   (317) 264-2820
- Indiana Small Business Development Centers   (317) 264-6871

Financial Assistance
- Indiana Development Finance Authority   (317) 233-4332

Minority/Women
- Women and Minority Business Assistance Program   (317) 264-2820
- Minority Business Development Divisions   (317) 232-3061

Indiana State Chamber of Commerce, Inc.   (317) 264-3110
One North Capitol St., Suite 200, Indianapolis, In 46204-2248

SBA District Office
429 North Pennsylvania, Suite 100, Indianapolis, IN 46204-1873

Indiana Small Business Development Centers
Indiana Small Business Development Center   (317) 261-3030
One North Capital, Suite 420, Indianapolis, IN 46204-2248

Bloomington	(812) 339-8937	Lafayette	(317) 742-2394
Columbus	(812) 372-6480	Madison	(812) 265-3127
Evansville	(812) 425-7232	Muncie	(317) 284-8144
Fort Wayne	(219) 426-0040	Portage	(219) 762-1696
Jeffersonville	(812) 288-6451	Richmond	(317) 962-2887
Kokomo	(317) 454-7922	Terre Haute	(812) 237-7676

Indiana Small Business Investment Companies
Indianapolis-Cambridge Ventures, LP   (317) 469-9704
South Bend-1st Source Capital Corporation   (219) 235-2180

Indiana Certified Development Companies
Evansville-Metro Small Business Assistance Corporation   (812) 426-5857
Fort Wayne-Community Development Corp. of Fort Wayne   (219) 427-1127
Hammond-Hammond Development Corporation   (219) 853-6399
Indianapolis-Indiana Statewide Certified Development Corp.   (317) 469-6166
Indianapolis-Mid City Pioneer Corporation   (317) 974-0504
Portage-Northwest Indiana Regional Development Corp.   (219) 763-6303
South Bend-Business Development Corp. of South Bend   (219) 235-9278

Micro Loans
Evansville-Metro Small Business Assistance   (812) 426-5857
Indianapolis-Eastside Community Investment   (317) 637-7300

IOWA

Statewide Financing Information and Resources: **www.state.ia.us**

Department of Economic Development   **(515) 242-4700**
200 East Grand Avenue, Des Moines, IA 50309

Economic Development
- Center for Industrial Research and Service   (515) 294-3420
- Marketing and Business Expansion Bureau   (515) 242-4735
- Office of Ombudsman   (515) 281-3592
- Small Business Bureau   (515) 242-4750
- Small Business Helpline   (515) 532-1216
- Small Business Workforce Development   (515) 281-9013

Financial Assistance
- Economic Development Set-Aside   (515) 242-4831
- Iowa Seed Capital Corporation   (515) 242-4860

Minority/Women
- Linked Investments for Tomorrow Program   (515) 281-3287
- Targeted Small Business Financial Assistance Program   (515) 242-4813
- Targeted Small Business Program   (515) 242-4721
- Entrepreneurs with Disabilities Program   (515) 242-4948
- Self-Employment Loan Program   (515) 242-4793

Iowa Association of Business & Industry   (515) 244-6149
904 Walnut Street, Suite 100, Des Moines, IA 50309-3503

SBA District Office
Cedar Rapids   (319) 362-6405
    215 Fourth Avenue, SE, Suite 200, Cedar Rapids, IA 52401-1806
Des Moines   (515) 284-4422
    210 Walnut Street, Room 749, Des Moines, IA 50309-2186

Iowa Small Business Development Centers
Iowa State University   (515) 292-6351
College of Business Administration
137 Lynn Avenue, Ames, IA 50014-7126

Ames	(515) 296-7828	Fort Dodge	(800) 362-2793
Audubon	(712) 563-2623	Iowa City	(319) 335-3742
Cedar Falls	(319) 273-2696	Marion	(319) 377-8256
Council Bluffs	(712) 325-3260	Mason City	(315) 422-4342
Creston	(515) 782-4161	Ottumwa	(515) 683-5127
Davenport	(319) 322-4499	Sioux City	(712) 274-6418
Des Moines	(515) 271-2655	Spencer	(712) 262-4213
Dubuque	(319) 588-3350	West Burlington	(319) 752-2731

Iowa Small Business Investment Companies
Cedar Rapids-MorAmerica Capital Corporation   (319) 363-8249

Iowa Certified Development Companies

Des Moines-Corp. for Economic Development in Des Moines	(515) 283-4004
Dubuque-ECIA Business Growth, Inc.	(515) 556-4166
Sioux City-Siouxland Economic Development Corporation	(712) 279-6286
Waterloo-Black Hawk County Econ. Devel. Committee, Inc.	(319) 235-2960
West Des Moines-Iowa Business Growth Company	(515) 223-4511

Micro Loans

Sioux City-Siouxland Economic Development	(712) 279-6286

KANSAS

Statewide Financing Information and Resources: **www.state.ks.us**

Department of Commerce   **(913) 296-3481**
700 SW Harrison Street, Suite 1300, Topeka, KS 66603-3712

Economic Development
- Administration Division   (913) 296-3481
- Kansas Technology Enterprise Corporation   (913) 296-5272

Financial Assistance
- Certified Development Companies   (316) 683-4422
- Power Certified Development Companies   (316) 267-3036
- Kansas Development Finance Authority   (913) 296-6747
- Kansas Venture Capital, Inc.   (913) 262-7117

Minority/Women
- Office of Minority

Kansas Chamber of Commerce & Industry   (913) 357-6321
835 SW Topeka Blvd., Topeka, KS 66612-1671

SBA District Office   (316) 269-6616
100 East English Street, Suite 510, Wichita, KS 67202

Kansas Small Business Development Centers
Wichita State University   (316) 978-3193
1845 Fairmount, Wichita, KS 67260-0148

Chanute	(316) 431-2820	Liberal	(316) 624-1951
Coffeyville	(316) 251-7700	Manhattan	(316) 532-5529
Dodge City	(316) 227-9247	Overland Park	(913) 469-3878

Fort Scott	(316) 223-2700	Parsons	(316) 421-6700
Garden City	(316) 276-9632	Pittsburg	(316) 235-4920
Hays	(913) 628-5340	Pratt	(316) 672-5641
Hutchinson	(316) 665-4950	Salina	(913) 826-2616
Independence	(316) 332-1420	Topeka	(913) 231-1010

Kansas Small Business Investment Company
Overland Park-Kansas Venture Capital   (913) 262-7117

Kansas Certified Development Companies
Dodge City-Great Plains Development, Inc.   (316) 227-6406
Emporia-Eastern Kansas Economic Development Group, Inc. (316) 342-7041
Hill City-Pioneer Country Development, Inc.   (913) 674-3488
Kansas City-Avenue Area Incorporated   (913) 371-0065
Kansas City-Citywide Development Corporation   (913) 573-5733
Lawrence-Wakarusa Valley Development, Inc.   (913) 865-4425
Overland Park-Johnson County Development Co.   (913) 599-1717
Pittsburg-Mid-America. Inc.   (316) 235-4920
Topeka-Topeka/Shawnee County Development Corporation (913) 368-3711
Wichita-South Central Kansas Economic Devel. District, Inc. (316) 683-4422

Micro Loans
Kansas City-Center for Business Innovation   (816) 561-8567
Wichita-South Central Kansas EDC   (316) 683-4422

KENTUCKY

Statewide Financing Information and Resources: www.state.ky.us

Kentucky Cabinet for Economic Development   (502) 564-7140
2300 Capital Plaza Tower, Frankfort, KY 40601

Economic Development
• Business Information Clearinghouse   (502) 564-4252
• Office of Business and Technology   (502) 564-4252
• University of Kentucky's Management Center   (606) 257-8746

Financial Assistance
• Commonwealth Small Business Development Corporation (502) 564-4320
• Kentucky Department of Financial Incentives   (502) 564-4554
• Kentucky Investment Capital Network   (502) 564-7140

Minority/Women
- Small and Minority Business Division   (502) 564-2064

Kentucky Chamber of Commerce   (502) 695-4700
464 Chenault Road, P.O. Box 817, Frankfort, KY 40602

SBA District Office
600 Dr., M.I. King Jr. Place, Room 188, Louisville, KY 40202

Kentucky Small Business Development Centers
University of Kentucky   (606) 257-7668
Center for Business Development
225 Business and Economics Building, Lexington, KY 40506-0034

Ashland	(606) 329-8011	Bowling Green	(502) 745-1905
Middlesboro	(606) 242-2145	Elizabethtown	(502) 765-6737
Morehead	(606) 783-2895		
Highland Heights	(606) 572-2856	Murray	(502) 762-2856
Hopkinsville	(502) 886-8666	Owensboro	(502) 926-8085
Lexington	(606) 257-7666	Pikeville	(606) 432-5848
Louisville	(502) 574-4770	Somerset	(606) 677-6120

Kentucky Small Business Investment Companies
London-Mountain Ventures, Inc.   (606) 878-6635
Louisville-Equal Opportunity Finance, Inc.   (502) 423-1943

Kentucky Certified Development Companies
Ashland-Boyd Greenup Economic Development Corp.   (606) 324-5113
Bowling Green-Barren River Development Council   (502) 781-2381
Florence-Northern Kentucky Area Development District, Inc. (606) 283-1885
Frankfort-Commonwealth Small Business Devel. Corp.   (502) 564-4554
Hopkinsville-Pennyrile Area Development District, Inc.   (502) 886-9484
Lexington-Urban County community Development Corp.   (606) 258-3131
Louisville-Metropolitan Capital Access Corporation   (502) 574-3051
Mayfield-Purchase Area Development District   (502) 247-7171

Micro Loans
Louisville-Louisville Central Development   (502) 583-8821
Lexington-Community Ventures   (606) 231-0054

LOUISIANA

Statewide Financing Information and Resources: www.state.la.us

Department of Economic Development   (504) 342-3000
P.O. Box 94185, Baton Rouge, LA 70804

Economic Development
- Office of Commerce and Industry   (504) 342-5893
  Division of Business Services

Financial Assistance
- Office of Commerce and Industry, Financial Incentives   (504) 342-5398
- Louisiana Economic Development Corporation   (504) 342-5675

Minority/Women
- Division of Minority and Women's Business Enterprise   (504) 342-5373

Louisiana Association of Business & Industry   (504) 928-5388
P.O. Box 80258, Baton Rouge, LA 70898-0258

SBA District Office   (504) 589-2354
365 Canal Street, Suite 2250, New Orleans, LA 70130

Louisiana Small Business Development Centers
Northeast Louisiana University   (318) 342-5506
College of Business Administration, Room 2-57, Monroe, LA 71209-6435

Alexandria	(318) 484-2123		
New Orleans (UNO)	(504) 539-9292		
Baton Rouge	(504) 922-0998	(Loyola U.)	(504) 863-3474
Hammond	(504) 549-3831	(So. U.)	(504) 286-5308
Lafayette	(318) 262-5344	Ruston	(318) 257-3537
Lake Charles	(318) 475-5520	Shreveport	(318) 797-5144
Monroe	(318) 342-1224	Thibodaux	(504) 448-4242
Natchitoches	(318) 357-5611		

Louisiana Small Business Investment Company
Baton Rouge-Premier Venture Capital Corporation   (504) 332-4421
New Orleans-First Commerce Capital   (504) 623-1600

Louisiana Certified Development Companies
Alexandria-Kisatchie-Delta Regional Planning and Devel.   (318) 487-5454

Lafayette-Louisiana Capital Certified Development Co., Inc.	(318) 234-2977
Metairie-JEDCO Development Corporation	(504) 830-4860
Monroe-Northeast Louisiana Industries, Inc.	(318) 323-0878
New Orleans-Regional Business Development Loan Corp.	(504) 524-6172
Shreveport-Ark-La-Tex Investment & Development Corp.	(318) 632-2022

Micro Loans

Jennings-Greater Jennings Chamber of Commerce	(318) 824-0933

MAINE

Statewide Financing Information and Resources:	**www.state.me.us**

Department of Economic and Community Development	**(207) 287-2656**
State House Station #59	
Augusta, ME, 04333-0949	

Economic Development

• Office of Business Development	(207) 287-3153
• Business Answers	(207) 287-3153
Toll-Free in Maine	(800) 872-3838
Toll-free out of state	(800) 541-5872

Financial Assistance

• Finance Authority of Maine	(207) 623-3263
• Linked Investment Program	(207) 623-3263

Maine Chamber of Commerce & Industry	(207) 623-4568
7 Community Drive, Augusta, ME 04330-9412	

SBA District Office	(207) 622-8378
40 Western Avenue, Room 512, Augusta, ME 04330	

Maine Small Business Development Centers

University of Southern Maine			(207) 780-4420
93 Falmouth Street, P.O. Box 9300, Portland, ME 04104-9300			
Auburn	(207) 783-9186	Portland	(207) 780-4949
Augusta	(207- 621-0243	Bangor	(207) 942-6389
Sanford	(207) 324-0316	Brunswick	(207) 882-4340
Caribou	(207) 498-8736	Wiscasset	(207) 882-4340
Machias	(207) 255-0983		

Maine Small Business Investment Company
Portland-North Atlantic Venture Fund II   (207) 772-1001

Maine Certified Development Companies
Auburn-Androscoggin Valley Council of Governments   (207) 783-9186
Bangor-Eastern Maine Development Corporation   (207) 942-6389
Wiscasset-Coastal Enterprises, Inc.   (207) 882-7552

Micro Loans
Caribou-Northern Maine Development   (207) 498-8736
Wiscasset-Coastal Enterprises   (207) 882-7552

MARYLAND

Statewide Financing Information and Resources: www.state.md.us

Department of Economic and Business Development   **(410) 767-6300**
Redwood Tower, 217 East Redwood St., Baltimore, MD 21202

Economic Development
• Office of Regional Response   (410) 767-0523
• At-Risk Business   (410) 767-6517
• SBDC Network   (410) 767-6552

Financial Assistance
• Maryland Small Business Development Financing Authority (410) 767-6539

Minority/Women
• Office of Minority Affairs   (410) 767-8232
• Procurement Office   (410) 767-7215

Maryland Chamber of Commerce   (410) 269-0642
60 West Street, Suite 100, Annapolis, MD 21401

SBA District Office   (410) 962-4392
10 South Howard Street, Room 6220, Baltimore, MD 21202

Maryland Small Business Development Centers
University of Maryland, College Park   (301) 403-8300
Annapolis   (410) 224-4205   Landover   (301) 883-6491
Baltimore   (410) 659-1930   McHenry   (301) 387-3080

Bel Air	(410) 893-3837	Owings Mills	(410) 356-2888
Columbia	(410) 313-6550	Rockville	(301) 217-2345
Cumberland	(301) 724-6716	Salisbury	(410) 546-4325
Elkton	(410) 392-0597	Towson	(410) 832-5866
Frederick	(301) 846-2683	Waldorf	(301) 934-7583
Great Mills	(301) 863-6679	Westminster	(410) 857-8166
Hagerstown	(301) 797-0327	Wye Mills	(410) 827-5286

Maryland Small Business Investment Companies
Baltimore-Anthem Capital, LP   (410) 625-1510
Bethesda-Security Financial and Investment Corporation   (301) 951-4288
Silver Spring-Syncom Capital Corporation   (301) 608-3207

Maryland Certified Development Companies
Baltimore-Mid-Atlantic Business Finance Corporation   (410) 539-2449
Largo-Prince George's County Financial Services Corp.   (301) 386-5600

Micro Loans
Baltimore-Council for Economic Business Opportunities   (410) 576-2326

MASSACHUSETTS

Statewide Financing Information and Resources: **www.state.ma.us**

Office of Business Development   **(617) 727-3206**
One Ashburton Place, Room 2101, Boston, MA 02108

Economic Development
• Massachusetts Business Development Corporation   617) 350-8877

Financial Assistance
• Massachusetts Industrial Finance Authority   (617) 451-2477
• Capital Formation Service   (617) 552-4091
• Technology Capital Network, Inc.   (617) 253-7163

Minority/Women
State Office ofMinority and Women's Business Assistance   (617) 727-8692

West Suburban Chamber of Commerce   (617) 894-4700
One Moody Street, Suite 301, Waltham, MA 02154

SBA District Office -Boston   (617) 565-5590
10 Causeway Street, Room 265, Boston, MA 02222-1093
Springfield (Branch Office)   (413) 785-0268
1550 Main Street, Room 212, Boston, MA01103

Massachusetts Small Business Development Centers
University of Massachusetts   (413) 545-6301
Room 205, School of Management, Amherst, MA 01003
Boston (Minority Business Assistance Center)   (617) 287-7750
Springfield   (413) 737-6712   Chestnut Hill   (617) 552-4091
Worcester   (508) 793-7615

Massachusetts Small Business Investment Companies
Boston-BancBoston Ventures, Inc.   (617) 434-2442
Boston-Chestnut Street Partners, Inc.   (617) 345-7200
Boston-Commonwealth Enterprise Fund, Inc.   (617) 482-1881
Boston-Northeast SBI Corp.   (617) 445-2100
Boston-Pioneer Ventures Limited Partnership   (617) 742-7825
Boston-Pioneer Ventures Limited Partnership II   (617) 422-4947
Boston-Transportation Capital Corporation   (617) 536-0344
Boston-U.S. Trust Capital Corporation   (617) 726-7000
Cambridge-Zero Stage Capital V, LP   (617) 876-5355
Danvers-Seacoast, LP   (508) 777-3866
Farmington-Argonauts MESBIC Corporation   (508) 820-3430
Newton-Business Achievement Corporation   (617) 965-0550

Massachusetts Certified Development Companies
Boston-Massachusetts Certified Development Corporation   (617) 350-8877
Holyoke-Riverside Development Corporation   (413) 533-7102
Leominster-North Central Mass. Development Corp.   (508) 840-4300 x236
Lynn-Lynn Capital Investment Corporation   (617) 592-2361
Peabody-Northeastern Mass. Economic Development Co.   (508) 531-0454
Pittsfield-Pittsfield Economic Revitalization Corporation   (413) 499-9371
Quincy-South Shore Economic Development Corporation   (617) 479-1111
Springfield-Western Mass. Small Business Assistance, Inc.   (413) 787-1553
Taunton-South Eastern Economic Development Corporation   (508) 822-1020
Waltham-Bay Colony Development   (617) 891-3594
Worcester-Worcester Business Development Corporation   (508) 753-2924

Micro Loans
Boston-Jewish Vocational Service   (617) 451-8147
Springfield-Springfield Business Development   (413) 787-6050

MICHIGAN

Statewide Financing Information and Resources: www.state.mi.us

Michigan Jobs Commission   **(517) 373-9808**
Victor Office Center, Fourth Floor, 201 N. Washington Square
Lansing, MI 48913

Economic Development
- Business Start-up Assistance   (517) 373-9808
- Economic/Labor Market Information   (517) 373-9808

Financial Assistance
- Business Operating Cost Estimating Service   (517) 373-9808
- Joint Venture Assistance   (517) 373-9808
- Private Financing Referral Service   (517) 373-9808
- Public Financing Programs   (517) 373-9808

Minority/Women
- Minority and Women-Owner Business Services   (517) 373-9808

Michigan Chamber of Commerce   (517) 371-2100
600 South Walnut Street, Lansing, MI 48933

SBA District Offices-Detroit   (313) 226-6075
477 Michigan Avenue, Room 515, Detroit, MI 48226
Marquette (Branch Office)   (906) 225-1108
228 West Washington, Suite 11, Marquette, MI 49885

Michigan Small Business Development Centers
Wayne State University   (313) 964-1798
2727 Second Avenue, Room 107, Detroit, MI 48201

Allendale	(616) 892-4120	Howell	(517) 546-4020
Ann Arbor	(313) 930-0033	Bad Axe	(517) 269-6431
Lansing	(517) 483-1921	Benton Harbor	(616) 927-8179
Lapeer	(810) 667-0080	Big Rapids	(616) 592-3553
Brighton	(810) 227-3556	Mt. Pleasant	(517) 774-3270
Cadillac	(616) 775-9776	Muskegon	(616) 722-3751
Caro	(517) 673-2849	Detroit	(313) 993-1115
Saline	(313) 944-1016	Escanaba	(906) 786-9234
Traverse City	(616) 929-5000	Flint	(810) 239-5847
Grand Haven	(616) 846-3153	Troy	(810) 952-5800
Grand Rapids	(616) 771-6693	Hart	(616) 873-7141
Warren	(810) 751-3939	Highland Park	(313) 222-2956

Michigan Small Business Investment Companies

Ann Arbor-White Pines Capital Corporation	(313) 747-9401
Dearborn-Dearborn Capital Corporation	(313) 337-8577
Farmington Hills-Metro District Investments	(810) 851-6300
Lansing-The Capital Fund	(517) 323-7772

Michigan Certified Development Companies

Big Rapids-Growth Finance Corporation	(616) 592-2082
Detroit-Detroit Economic Growth Corporation	(313) 963-2940
Detroit-Metropolitan Growth and Development Corporation	(313) 224-0749
Grand Rapids-Economic Development Foundation	(616) 785-4333
Holland-Ottawa County Development Company, Inc.	(616) 892-4120
Lansing-Michigan Certified Development	(517) 373-6379
Lapeer-Lapeer Development Corporation	(810) 667-0080
Saginaw-East Central Michigan Development Corporation	(517) 797-0800

Micro Loans

Detroit-Detroit Economic Growth	(312) 963-2940
Flint-Community Capital	(810) 239-5847

MINNESOTA

Statewide Financing Information and Resources: **www.state.mn.us**

Small Business Assistance Office **(612) 296-3871**
500 Metro Square, 121 7th Place East, St. Paul, MN 55101-2146

Economic Development
- Bureau of Small Business   (612) 296-3871
- Small Business Development Center (Administrative Ofc.)   (612) 297-5770

Financial Assistance
- Department of Trade and Economic Development   (612) 297-1391
  Office of Business Development & Finance

Minnesota Chamber of Commerce   (612) 292-4650
30 East Seventh Street, Suite 1700, St. Paul, MN 55101

SBA District Office   (612) 370-2324
100 North Sixth Street, Suite 610-C, Minneapolis, MN 55403-1563

Minneapolis Small Business Development Centers

Department of Trade and Economic Development   (612) 297-5770
500 Metro Square, 121 Seventh Place East, St. Paul, MN 55101-2146

Bemidji	(218) 755-4286	Moorhead	(218) 236-2289
Bloomington	(612) 832-6221	Brainerd	(218) 828-2528
Pine City	(612) 629-7340	Duluth	(218) 726-6192
Plymouth	(612) 550-7218	Grand Rapids	(218) 327-2241
Hibbing	(218) 262-6703	Rochester	(507) 285-7536
International Falls	(218) 285-2255	Rosemount	(612) 423-8262
Mankato	(507) 389-8863	Marshall	(507) 537-7386
St. Cloud	(320) 255-4842	Minneapolis	(612) 338-3280
Virginia	(218) 741-4251		

Minnesota Small Business Investment Companies

Duluth-Northland Capital Venture Partnership	(218) 722-0545
Minneapolis-Agio Capital	(612) 339-8408
Minneapolis-Capital Dimensions Venture Fund, Inc.	(612) 854-3007
Minneapolis-Milestone Growth Fund, Inc	(612) 338-0090
Minneapolis-Norwest Equity Partners, IV, LP	(612) 667-1650
Minneapolis-Norwest Equity Partners V, LP	(612) 667-1650
Minneapolis-Piper Jaffray Healthcare Capital LP	(612) 342-6335

Minnesota Certified Development Companies

Arden Hills-Twin Cities Metro Certified Development Co.	(612) 481-8081
Coon Rapids-Central Minnesota Development Company	(612) 755-2304
Mankato-Region Nine Development Corporation	(507) 387-5643
Minneapolis-Economic Development Company	(612) 673-5176
Rochester-Southeastern Minnesota 504 Development, Inc.	(612) 288-6442
St. Cloud-Minnesota Business Finance, Inc.	(320) 255-1685
St. Paul-Saint Paul/Metro East Development Corporation	(612) 225-4900
Slayton-Prairieland Economic Development Corporation	(507) 836-6656

Micro Loans

Minneapolis-Women Venture	(612) 646-3808
Minneapolis-Consortium of Community Development	(612) 371-9986

MISSISSIPPI

Statewide Financing Information and Resources: **www.state.ms.us**

**Mississippi Department of Economic and
   Community Development**   **(601) 359-3449**
P.O. Box 849, Jackson MS 39205-0849

Economic Development
- Business Incubator   (601) 352-0957
- Existing Business and Industry Assistance Division   (601) 359-3593
- Mississippi Enterprise for Technology   (601) 688-3144

Financial Assistance
- Mississippi Business Finance Corporation   (601) 359-3552

Minority/Women
- Jackson Minority Business Development Center   (601) 362-2260
- Minority Business Enterprise   (601) 359-3448

Mississippi Economic Council   (601) 969-0022
620 North Street, P.O. Box 23276, Jackson, MS39225-3276

SBA District Office   (601) 863-4449
    One Hancock Plaza, Gulfport, MS 39501-7758
Jackson   (601) 965-4378
    101 West Capitol Street, Suite 400, Jackson, MS 39201

Mississippi Small Business Development Centers
University of Mississippi   (601) 232-5001
Old Chemistry Building, Suite 216 University, MS 38677

Biloxi	(601) 396-1288	Booneville	(601) 720-7448
Cleveland	(601) 846-4236	Decatur	(601) 635-2111
Ellisville	(601) 477-4165	Gautier	(601) 497-7723
Greenville	(601) 378-8183	Hattiesburg	(601) 544-0030
Itta Bena	(601) 254-3601	Jackson	(601) 968-2795
Long Beach	(601) 865-4578	Lorman	(601) 877-6684
Meridan	(601) 482-7445	Mississippi State	(601) 325-8684
Natchez	(601) 445-5254	Raymond	(601) 857-3536
Ridgeland	(601) 865-4578	Southaven	(601) 342-7648
Summit	(601) 276-3890	Tupelo	(601) 680-8515
University	(601) 234-2120		

Mississippi Small Business Investment Company
Greenville-Sun Delta Access Center, Inc.   (601) 335-5291

Mississippi Certified Development Companies
Gulfport-Southern Mississippi Economic Devel. Co., Inc.   (601) 868-2311
Jackson-Mississippi Development Company   (601) 981-1625
Pontotoc-Three Rivers local Development Company, Inc.   (601) 489-2415

Micro Loans

Greenville-Delta Foundation	(601) 335-5291
Jackson-Friends at Children of Mississippi	(601) 362-1541

MISSOURI

Statewide Financing Information and Resources: www.state.mo.us

Missouri Department of Economic Development   **(573) 751-4962**
Truman State Office Building
301 West High Street, P.O. Box 1157
Jefferson City, MO 65102

Economic Development
* Business Development Section   (573) 751-9045
* Business Information Programs   (573) 751-4982

Financial Assistance
* Community and Economic Development   (573) 751-0717
  Finance Program

Minority/Women
* Office of Minority Business   (573) 751-3237
* Women's Council   (573) 751-0810

Missouri Chamber of Commerce   (573) 634-3511
P.O. Box 149, Jefferson City, MO 65102

SBA District Offices-Kansas City   (816) 374-6708
    Lucas Place, 323 West Eighth St, Suite 501, Kansas City, MO 64105
St. Louis   (314) 539-6600
    815 Olive Street, Room 242, St. Louis, MO63101
Springfield (Branch Office)   (417) 864-7670
    620 South Glenstone St., Suite 110, Springfield, MO 65802-3200

Missouri Small Business Development Centers
University of Missouri   (573) 882-0344
300 University Place, Columbia, MO 65211

Cape Girardeau	(573) 290-5965	Chillicothe	(816) 646-6920
Columbia	(314) 882-7096	Flat River	(573) 431-4593
Joplin	(417) 625-9313	Kansas City	(816) 501-4572
Kirksville	(816) 785-4307	Rolla	(573) 341-4559

| Springfield | (417) 836-5685 | St. Louis | (314) 977-7232 |
| Warrensburg | (816) 543-4402 | | |

Missouri Small Business Investment Companies

Clayton Enterprise Fund	(314) 725-5500
Kansas City-Bankers Capital Corporation	(816) 531-1600
Kansas City-Capital for Business Venture Fund II,LP	(816) 234-2357
Kansas City-KCEP	(816) 960-1771
Kansas City-MorAmerica Capital Corporation	(816) 842-0114
Kansas City-United Missouri Capital Corporation	(816) 860-7914
St. Louis-Capital for Business Venture Fund I, Inc.	(314) 746-7427
St. Louis-Gateway Partners, LP	(314) 721-5707

Missouri Certified Development Companies

Camdenton-Central Ozarks Development, Inc.	(573) 346-5692
Clayton-Business Finance Corporation of St. Louis County	(314) 889-7663
Columbia-Enterprise Development Corporation	(573) 875-8117
Jefferson City-Rural Missouri, Inc.	(573) 635-0136
Kansas City-Clay Development Corporation	(816) 468-4989
Kansas City-Economic Development Corp. of Kansas City	(816) 221-0636
Hillsboro-Economic Development Corp. of Jefferson County	(314) 789-5336
Rolla-Meramec Regional Development	(573) 364-2993
St. Charles-St. Charles EDC	(314) 441-6880
St. Joseph-Mo-Kan Development, Inc.	(816) 233-3144
St. Louis-St. Louis Local Development Company	(314) 622-3400
Trenton-Green Hills Rural Development. Inc.	(816) 359-5086

Micro Loans

Kansas City-Center for Business Innovation	(816) 561-8567

MONTANA

Statewide Financing Information and Resources:	**www.state.mt.us**

Department of Commerce	**(406) 444-3494**
1424 Ninth Avenue, Helena, MT 59620-0501	

Economic Development
- Economic Development Division   (406) 444-3814
- Business Recruitment Program   (406) 444-4187

Financial Assistance
- Microbusiness Finance Program   (406) 444-4187

- Board of Investments   (406) 444-0001
- CDBG Economic Development Program   (406) 444-2787

Minority/Women
- Disadvantaged Business and Women's
  Business Procurement Assistance   (406) 444-6337

SBA District Office   (406) 441-1081
301 South Park, Drawer 10054, Room 334, Helena, MT 59626

Montana Small Business Development Centers
Montana Department of Commerce (406) 444-4780
1424 North Avenue, Helena, MT 59620

Billings	(406) 256-6875	Kalispell	(406) 756-3833
Bozeman	(406) 587-3113	Missoula	(406) 543-3550
Butte	(406) 782-7333	Sidney	(406) 482-5024
Cedar Falls-High Plains Development			(406) 454-1934
Havre	(406) 265-9226		
Helena-Small Business Development Service			(406) 444-4780

Montana Certified Development Companies
Billings-Economic Devel. Corp. of Yellowstone County   (406) 245-0415
Helena-Montana community Finance Corp.   (406) 443-3261

Micro Loans   None

NEBRASKA

Statewide Financing Information and Resources: www.state.ne.us

Nebraska Department of Economic Development   **(402) 471-3111**
P.O. Box 94666, 301 Centennial Mall South, Lincoln, NE 68509-4666

Economic Development
- Existing Business Assistance Division   (402) 471-4167
- One-Stop Business Assistance Center   (402) 471-3782
- Nebraska Business Development Center   (402) 595-2381
- Entrepreneurship Projects   (402) 471-4803

Financial Assistance
- Export Promotion   (402) 471-4668
- Nebraska investment Finance Authority   (402) 434-3900

Minority/Women
- Office of Women's Business Ownership   (402) 221-3622

Nebraska Chamber of Commerce & Industry   (402) 474-4422
1320 Lincoln Mall, P.O. Box 95128, Lincoln, NE 68509

SBA District Office   (402) 221-3622
11141 Mill Valley Road, Omaha, NE 68154

Nebraska Small Business Development Centers
University of Nebraska at Omaha   (402) 554-2541
College of Business Administration Bldg.
60th & Dodge Streets, Room 407, Omaha, NE 68182

Chadron	(308) 432-6286	Omaha	(402) 595-3511
Kearney	(308) 865-8344	Omaha (U. of NE)	(402) 595-2391
Lincoln	(402) 472-3358	Peru	(402) 872-2274
North Platte	(308) 635-7513	Scottsbluff	(308) 635-7513
Wayne	(402) 375-7575		

Nebraska Certified Development Company
Lincoln-Nebraska Economic Development Corporation   (402) 475-2795

Micro Loans
Omaha-Small Business Network   (402) 346-8262

NEVADA

Statewide Financing Information and Resources: www.state.nv.us

Nevada State Development Corporation   **(702) 323-3625**
350 South Central Street, Suite 310, Reno, NV 89501

Economic Development
- Nevada Department of Business and Industry   (702) 486-2750
- Nevada State Development Corporation   (702) 323-3625
- Nevada Self-Employment Trust (NSET)   (702) 329-6789

Financial Assistance
- Department of Business and Industry   (702) 687-4250
  Industrial Development Revenue Bond Program
- Southern Nevada Certified Development Company   (702) 732-3998
- Nevada Revolving Loan Fund Program (702) 882-3882 or (702) 687-1812

- Nevada State Development Corporation (702) 323-3625
- Commission on Economic Development (702) 687-4325
- Nevada Development Capital Corporation (702) 323-3625

Minority/Women
- Nevada Department of Business and Industry (702) 486-2750

Nevada State Chamber of Commerce (702) 686-3030
405 Marsh Avenue, P.O. Box 3499, Reno, NV 89505

SBA District Office (702) 388-6611
301 E. Stewart St., Rm. 301, P.O. Box 7527, Las Vegas, NV 89125-2527

Nevada Small Business Development Centers
University of Nevada at Reno (702) 784-1717
College of Business Administration
Mail Stop 032, 1664 N. Virginia Street, Reno, NV 89503

Winnemucca	(702) 623-5777	Carson City (CoC)	(702) 882-1565
Las Vegas	(702) 895-0852	Elko (CC)	(702) 753-2245
North Las Vegas	(702) 399-6300	Incline Village (CoC)	(702) 831-4440

Small Business Investment Companies None

Nevada Certified Development Companies
Las Vegas-New Ventures Capital Development (702) 382-9522
Las Vegas-Southern Nevada Certified Development Corp. (702) 732-3998
Reno-Nevada State Development Corporation (702) 323-3625

NEW HAMPSHIRE

Statewide Financing Information and Resources: www.state.nh.us

Business Finance Authority **(603) 271-2391**
New Hampshire Industrial Development Authority
Four Park Street, Suite 302, Concord, NH 03301

Business Development
- Business Visitation Program (603) 271-2591
- Corporate Division (603) 271-3244
- New Hampshire Business Development Corporation (603) 623-5500
- Office of Business and Industrial Development (603) 271-2591

Financial Assistance
- Business Finance Authority (603) 271-2391
  Industrial Revenue Bonds
  Credit Enhancement Programs
- Office of Business and Industrial Development (603) 271-2591
- Technology Capital Network, Inc. (617) 253-7163

Business and Industry Association of New Hampshire   (603) 224-5388
122 North Main Street, Concord, NH 03301

SBA District Office
143 North Main St., Suite 202, P.O. Box 1258, Concord, NH 03302-1258

New Hampshire Small Business Development Centers
University of New Hampshire   (603) 862-2200
108 McConnell Hall, Durham, NH 03824
Keene   (603) 358-2602 Littleton   (603) 444-1053
Manchester   (603) 624-2000 Nashua   (603) 886-1233
Plymouth   (603) 535-2526

New Hampshire Certified Development Companies
Concord-Concord Regional Development corporation   (603) 228-1872
Portsmouth-Granite State Economic Development Corp.   (603) 436-0009

Micro Loans
Concord-Capital Regional Development   (603) 228-1872
Portsmouth-Granite State EDC   (603) 436-0009

NEW JERSEY

Statewide Financing Information and Resources: **www.state.nj.us**

New Jersey Department of Commerce and Economic Development
20 West State Street, CN 835, Trenton, NJ 08625   (609) 292-2444

Economic Development
- Prospect Marketing   (609) 292-0700

Financial Assistance
- New Jersey Economic Development Authority   (609) 292-1800
  -Commercial Lending   (609) 292-0187

Minority/Women
- Division of Development for Small Business and
  Women's and Minority Businesses   (609) 292-3860

New Jersey State Chamber of Commerce   (609) 989-7888
50 W. State Street, Suite 1310, Trenton, NJ 08608

SBA District Office   (201) 645-2434
2 Gateway Center, Fourth Floor, Newark, NJ 07102

New Jersey Small Business Development Centers
Rutgers University   (201) 648-5950
Graduate School of Management   (201) 648-5950
University Heights, 180 University Ave, Newark, NJ 07102
Atlantic City   (609) 345-5600   Trenton   (609) 586-4800
Camden   (609) 757-6221   Union   (908) 527-2946
Lincroft   (908) 842-8685   Washington   (908) 689-9620
Paramus   (201) 447-7841

New Jersey Small Business Investment Companies
Chatham-MidMark Capital, LP   (201) 822-2999
Fort Lee-Capital Circulation Corporation   (201) 947-8637
Little Falls-Tappan Zee Capital Corporation   (201) 256-8280
Livingston-CIT Group/Venture Capital, Inc.   (201) 740-5429
Newark-ESLO Capital Corporation   (201) 242-4488
Newark-Rutgers Minority Investment Company   (201) 648-5287
Summit-First Fidelity Capital   (908) 598-3363
Teaneck-DFW Capital Partners, LP   (201) 836-2233

New Jersey Certified Development Companies
Newark-Union County Economic Development Corporation (908) 527-1166
Trenton-Corporation for Business Assistance in New Jersey (609) 633-2631
West Orange- Economic Development Ciro, Essex County (201) 731-2772

Micro Loans
Newark-Greater Newark Business Development   (201) 242-6237
Trenton-Trenton Business Asst.   (609) 989-3509

NEW MEXICO

Statewide Financing Information and Resources:	**www.state.nm.us**

Economic Development Department   (505) 827-0300
P.O. Box 20003, Santa Fe, NM 87504-5003

Economic Development
• New Mexico Small Business Development Center   (505) 438-1362

Financial Assistance
• Economic Development Division   (505) 827-0300

Minority/Women
• Governor's Commission on the Status of Women   (505) 841-8920

Association of Commerce & Industry of New Mexico   (505) 842-0644
2309 Renard Place, SE, Suite 402, Albuquerque, NM 87106

SBA District Office   (505) 766-1870
625 Silver Avenue, SW, Suite 320, Albuquerque, NM 87102

New Mexico Small Business Development Centers
Santa Fe Community College   (505) 438-1362
P.O. Box 4187, South Richards Avenue, Santa Fe, NM 87502-4187

Alamogondo	(505) 434-5272	Los Alamos	(505) 662-0001
Albuquerque	(505) 248-0132	Los Lunas	(505) 925-8980
Carlsbad	(505) 887-6562	Las Vegas	(505) 454-2595
Clovis	(505) 769-4136	Roswell	(505) 624 7133
Espanola	(505) 747-2236	Silver City	(505) 538-6320
Farmington	(505) 599-0528	Gallup	(505) 722-2220
Tucumcaru	(505) 461-4413	Grants	(505) 287-8221
Las Cruces	(505) 527-7606	Hobbs	(505) 392-5549

New Mexico Certified Development Company
Albuquerque-Enchantment Land Certified Devel. Corp.   (505) 843-9232

Micro Loans
Albuquerque-Women's Economic Self-Sufficiency   (505) 848-4760

NEW YORK

Statewide Financing Information and Resources: www.state.ny.us

New York Empire State Development **(518) 473-0499**

Division for Small Business
One Commerce Plaza, Albany, NY 12245

Business Development
- Business Assistance Hot Line (800) 782-8369
- Business Service Ombudsman (518) 473-0499 or (212) 803-2289
- Division for Small Business (518) 473-0499
- New York State Small Business Advisory Board (518) 473-0499
- Small Business Advocacy Program (518) 473-0499 or (212) 803-2200

Financial Assistance
- Empire State Development Corporation (212) 803-3100

Minority Women
- Entrepreneurial Assistance Program (212) 803-2410
- Minority and Women's Business Division (212) 803-2410

Other Key New York Phone Numbers

Business Council of New York State (518) 465-7511
125 Washington Avenue, Albany, NY 12210

SBA District Offices
Buffalo (716) 551-4301
    111 West Huron Street, Room 1311, Buffalo, NY 14202
Elmira (Branch Office) (607) 734-8130
    333 East Water Street, Fourth Floor, Elmira, NY 14901
Melville (Branch Office) (516) 454-0750
    35 Pinelawn Road, Suite 207W, Melville, NY 11747
New York (212) 264-4355
    26 Federal Plaza, Room, 3100, New York, NY 10278
Rochester (Branch Office) (716) 263-6700
    100 State Street, Suite 410, Rochester, NY 14614
Syracuse (315) 448-0423
    100 South Clinton Street, Room 1073, Syracuse, NY 13261

New York Small Business Development Centers

State University of New York (SUNY)			(518) 443-5398
SUNY Plaza S-523, Albany, NY 12246			(800) 732-SBDC
Albany	(518) 442-5577	New York City	(212) 346-1900
Binghamton	(607) 777-4024	Niagara Falls	(716) 285-4793
Bronx	(718) 563-3570	Oswego	(315) 343-1545
Brooklyn	(718) 368-4619	Plattsburgh	(518) 562-4260
Buffalo	(716) 878-4030	Rochester	(716) 232-7310
Canton	(315) 386-7312	Sanborn	(716) 693-1910
Corning	(607) 962-9461	Southhampton	(516) 287-0059
Dobbs Ferry	(914) 674-7485	Staten Island	(718) 390-7645
Farmington	(516) 420-2765	Stony Brook	(516) 632-9070
Fishkill	(914) 897-2607	Suffern	(914) 356-0370
Geneseo	(716) 245-5429	Syracuse	(315) 492-3029
Geneva	(315) 781-1253	Utica	(315) 792-7546
Hempstead	(516) 564-8672	Waterton	(315) 782-9262
Jamaica	(718) 262-2880	White Plains	(914) 644-4116
Jamestown	(716) 665-5754	Kingston	(914) 339-0025

New York Small Business Investment Companies

Albany-NYBDC Capital Corporation	(518) 463-2268
Buffalo-M&T capital Corporation	(716) 848-3800
Flushing-FirstCounty Capital, Inc.	(718) 461-1778
Flushing-Flushing Capital Corporation	(718) 886-5866
Great Neck-Sterling Commercial Capital, Inc.	(516) 482-7374
Mount Kisco-KOCO Capital Co.	(914) 241-7430
New York-American Asian Capital Corporation	(212) 422-6880
New York-Argentum Capital Partners, LP	(212) 949-8272
New York-BT Capital Corporation	(212) 250-8082
New York-Barclays Capital	(212) 412-3937
New York-Capital Investors & Management Corporation	(212) 964-2480
New York-Chase Manhattan Capital Partners	(212) 662-3100
New York-Citicorp Venture Capital, LTD	(212) 559-1127
New York-Creditanstalt	(203) 861-1410
New York-East Coast Venture Capital, Inc.	(212) 245-6460
New York-Edwards Capitak Co. (Medallion Fin. Corp.)	(212) 682-3300
New York-Elk Associates Funding Corporation	(212) 355-2449
New York-Empire State Capital Corporation	(212) 513-1799
New York-Eos Partners SBIC, LP	(212) 832-5814
New York-Esquire Capital	(516) 462-6944
New York-Exeter Equity Partners, LP	(212) 872-1170
New York-Exeter Venture Lenders, LP	(212) 872-1170
New York-Exim Capital Corporation	(212) 683-3375

New York-Fair Capital Corporation	(212) 964-2480
New York-First Wall Street SBIC, LP	(212) 742-3770
New York-Freshstart Venture Capital Corporation	(212) 265-2249
New York-Furman Selz SBIC, LP	(212) 309-8200
New York-Hanam Capital Corporation	(212) 564-5225
New York-Inter Equity Capital Partners, LP	(212) 779-2022
New York-LEG Partners SBIC, LP	(212) 207-1585
New York-Medallion Funding Corporation	(212) 682-3300
New York-NatWest Capital	(212) 602-1200
New York-Norwood Venture Corporation	(212) 869-5075
New York-Paribas Principal, Inc.	(212) 841-2115
New York-Pierre Funding Corportion	(212) 888-1515
New York-Prospect Street	(212) 490-0480
New York-Pyramid Ventures, Inc.	(212) 250-9571
New York-Transportation Capital Corp. (Medallion Fin.)	(212) 682-3300
New York-Trusty Capital, Inc.	(212) 629-3011
New York-UBS Partners, Inc.	(212) 821-6490
New York-United Capital Investment Corporation	(212) 682-7210
New York-Venture Opportunities Corportion	(212) 832-3737
Purchase-International Paper Capital Formation, Inc.	(914) 397-1579
Rochester-Ibero American Investors Corporation	(716) 262-3440
Rye-Fundex Capital	(914) 967-2227
Tarrytown-TLC Funding Corporation	(914) 332-5200

New York Certified Development Companies

Albany-Albany Local Development Corporation	(518) 434-5192
Albany-Empire State Certified Development Corporation	(518) 463-2268
Binghamton Tier Information & Enterprises Resources, Inc.	(607) 724-1327
Buffalo-Buffalo Enterprise Development Corporation	(716) 842-6923
Carle Place-Long Island Development Corporation	(516) 349-7800
Hudson-Hudson Development Company	(518) 828-4718
Jamestown-Chautauqua Region Industrial Development Corp.	(716) 664-3262
Mohawk-Mohawk Valley Certified Development Corp.	(315) 866-4671
Oswego-Operation Oswego County, Inc.	(315) 343-1545
Port Jervis-Progress Development Corporation	(914) 858-8358
Rochester-Monroe County Industrial Development Corp.	(716) 428-5060
Rochester-Rochester Economic Development Corporation	(716) 428-6966
Saranac Lake-Adirondack Economic Development Corp.	(518) 891-5523
Syracuse-Greater Syracuse Business Development Corp.	(315) 470-1887

Micro Loans

New York-Manhattan BoroughDevelopment	(212) 791-3660
Rochester-Rural Opportunities	(716) 546-7180

NORTH CAROLINA

Statewide Financing Information and Resources: www.state.nc.us

North Carolina Small Business and Technology   (919) 715-7272
Development Center
333 Fayetteville Street Mall, Raleigh, NC 27603

Economic Development
• North Carolina Small Business and Technology   (919) 715-7272
  Development Center

Financial Assistance
• North Carolina Small Business and Technology   (919) 715-7272
  Development Center

North Carolina Citizens for Business & Industry   (919) 836-1400
225 Hillsborough Street, Suite 460, P.O. Box 2508, Raleigh, NC 27602

SBA District Office   (704) 344-6563
208 North College St., Suite A2015, Charlotte, NC 28202-2137

North Carolina Small Business Development Centers
University of North Carolina   (919) 715-7272
333 Fayette Street Mall, Suite 1150, Raleigh, NC 27601-1742   (800) 258-0862

Ashville	(704) 251-6025	Greensboro	(910) 334-7005
Boone	(704) 262-2492	Greenville	(919) 328-6183
Chapel Hill	(919) 962-0389	Hickory	(704) 345-1110
Charlotte	(704) 548-1090	Pembroke	(910) 521-6603
Cullowhee	(704) 227-7494	Rocky Mount	(919) 985-5130
Elizabeth City	(919) 335-3247	Wilmington	(910) 395-3744
Fayetteville	(910) 486-1727	Winston-Salem	(910) 750-2030

North Carolina Small Business Investment Companies
Charlotte-NationsBanc Capital Corporation   (704) 386-8063
Greensboro-Blue Ridge Investors   (910) 370-0576
Raleigh-Oberlin   (914) 743-2544

North Carolina Certified Development Companies
Charlotte-Centralina Development Corporation, Inc.   (704) 372-2416
Charlotte-Charlotte Certified Development Corporation   (704) 373-0160
Durham-Self-Help Ventures Fund   (919) 956-4400
Henderson-Region K Certified Development Company, Inc.   (919) 492-2531

Hertford-Abemaele Development Authority	(919) 426-5755
Hickory-Region E Development Corporation	(704) 322-9191
New Bern-Neuse River Development Authority, Inc.	(919) 638-6724
Raleigh-Capital Economic Development Corporation	(919) 832-4524
Rutherfordton-Region C Development Corporation, Inc.	(704) 287-2281
Waynesville-Smokey Mountain Development Corporation	(704) 452-1967
Wilmington-Wilmington Industrial Development, Inc.	(910) 763-8414
Winston-Salem-Northwest Piedmont Development Corp.	(910) 761-2108

Micro Loans

Boone-W.A.M.Y. Community Action	(704) 264-2421
Durham-Self-Help Ventures	(919) 956-8526

NORTH DAKOTA

Statewide Financing Information and Resources: www.state.nd.us

Department of Economic Development and Finance   **(701) 328-5300**
1833 East Dismarck Expresseway, Bismarck, ND 58504

Economic Development
- Business and Community Assistance Center
  Minot State University   (701) 858-3825
- Institute for Business and Industry Development   (701) 231-1001
- Center for Innovation and Business Development   (701) 777-3132

Financial Assistance
- Economic Development & Finance   (701) 328-5300

Minority/Women
- Native American Business Assistance   (701) 328-5300
- Women's Business Development   (701) 328-5300

Greater North Dakota Assn./State Chamber of Commerce   (701) 222-0929
2000 Schafer Street, P.O. Box 2639, Bismarck, ND 58502

SBA District Office   (701) 239-5131
657 2nd Avenue, North, Room 219, P.O. Box 3086, Fargo, ND 58108-3086

North Dakota Small Business Development Centers
University of North Dakota   (701) 777-3700
118 Gamble Hall, Grand Forks, ND 58202-7308   (800) 445-7232

Bismarck	(701) 223-8583	Dickinson	(701) 227-2096
Grand Forks	(701) 772-8502	Fargo (Regional)	(701) 237-0986
Minot	(701) 852-8861	Grafton	(800) 445-7232

North Dakota Small Business Investment Company
Fargo-North Dakota SBIC, LP   (701) 298-0003

North Dakota Certified Development Company
Fargo-Fargo-Cass Economic Development Center   (701) 237-6132

Micro Loans
Fargo-Lake Agassiz Regional   (701) 239-5373

OHIO

Statewide Financing Information and Resources: www.state.oh.us
Office of Small Business   **(614) 466-2718**
Ohio Department of Development
77 South High Street, P.O. Box 1001, Columbus, OH 43216-1001

Economic Development   (419) 332-2882
• One-Stop Business Permit Center

Financial Assistance
• Office of Minority Financial Incentives   (614) 644-7708
• Business Loans   (614) 466-5420

Minority/Women
• Women's Business Resource Program   (614) 466-4945
• Minority Business Development Program   (614) 466-5700

Ohio Chamber of Commerce   (614) 228-4201
230 East Town Street, P.O. Box 15159, Columbus, OH 43215-0154

SBA District Offices
Cincinnati (Branch Office)   (513) 684-2814
    525 Vine Street, Suite 870, Cincinnati, OH 45202
Cleveland   (216) 522-4180
    1111 Superior Avenue, Suite 630, Cleveland, OH 44114-2507
Columbus   (614) 469-6860
    2 Nationwide Plaza, Suite 1400, Columbus, OH 43215-2542

Ohio Small Business Development Centers
Ohio Department of Development (614) 466-2711
77 South High Street, P.O. Box 1001, Columbus, OH 43226-1001

Akron	(330) 379-3170	Lima	(419) 229-5320
Athens	(614) 592-1188	Lorian	(216) 233-6500
Bowling	(419) 352-3817	Marietta	(614) 376-4832
Canton	(216) 499-9600	Marion	(614) 387-0188
Celina	(419) 586-0355	New Philadelphia	(216) 339-9070
Cincinnati	(513) 753-7141	Portsmouth	(614) 355-2316
Cleveland	(216) 621-3300	Salem	(216) 332-0361
Cleveland	(216) 432-5364	Southpoint	(614) 894-3838
Columbus	(614) 225-6081	Springfield	(513) 322-7821
Dayton	(513) 226-8230	St. Clairsville	(614) 695-9678
Dayton	(513) 873-3503	Steubenville	(614) 282-6226
Defiance	(419) 784-3777	Toledo	(419) 243-8191
Fremont	(419) 334-8400	Youngstown	(216) 746-3350
Hillsboro	(513) 393-9599	Zanesville	(614) 452-4868
Jefferson	(216) 576-9134	Kettering	(513) 258-6180

Ohio Small Business Investment Companies

Cincinnati-River Cities Capital Fund, LP	(513) 621-9700
Cleveland-Clarion Capital Corporation	(216) 687-1096
Cleveland-Key Equity Capital Corporation	(216) 689-5776
Cleveland-National City Capital Corporation	(216) 575-2491
Columbus-Banc One Capital	(614) 227-4209
Dayton-Enterprise Ohio	(513) 226-0457
Worthington-Cactus Capital Company	(614) 436-4060

Ohio Certified Development Companies

Akron-Cascade Capital	(216) 376-5550
Canton-Stark Development Board Fianace Corporation	(330) 453-5900
Cincinnati-Cincinnati Local Development Company	(513) 352-1958
Cincinnati-Hamilton County Development Company, Inc.	(513) 632-8292
Cleveland-Cleveland Area Development Finance Corp.	(216) 621-3300
Columbus-Columbus Countywide Development Corp.	(614) 645-6171
Columbus-Ohio Statewide Development Corporation	(614) 466-5043
Dayton-Citywide Small Business Development Corp.	(513) 226-0457
Dayton-County Corp Development	(513) 225-6328
Franklin-Certified Devel. Corp. of Warren County, Inc.	(513) 748-4359
Hamilton-Certified Development Co. of Butler County, Inc.	(513) 887-3404
Mentor-Lake County Small Business Assistance Corporation	(216) 951-1290
Mentor-Mentor Economic Assistance Corporation	(216) 974-5739
Springfield-Clark County Development Corporation	(419) 243-8251

Xenia-Xenia-Greene County Small Business Devel. Co., Inc.   (513) 372-0444
Youngstown-Mahoning Valley Economic Development Corp.   (330) 759-3668

Micro Loans
Akron-Women's Entrepreneurial Growth   (330) 379-9280
Columbus-Columbus Countywide Development   (614) 645-6171

OKLAHOMA

Statewide Financing Information and Resources: **www.state.ok.us**

Oklahoma Department of Commerce   **(405) 843-9770**
6601 Broadway Extension, Building 5, Oklahoma City, OK 73116

Economic Development
- Business Development Division   (405) 841-5167
- Business Service Program   (405) 841-5227
- Research and Planning Division   (405) 841-5170
- Community Affairs and Development Division   (405) 841-9326

Financial Assistance
- Capital Resources Network   (405) 841-5140
- Oklahoma Development Finance Authority   (405) 848-9761

Minority/Women
- Minority Business Assistance   (405) 841-5227
- Women-Owned Certification   (405) 841-5242

Oklahoma State Chamber of Commerce & Industry   405) 235-3669
330 NE 10th Street, Oklahoma City, OK 73104

SBA District Office   (405) 231-5521
210 West Park Avenue, Suite 1300, Oklahoma City, OK 73102

Oklahoma Small Business Development Centers
Southern State University			(405) 924-0277
517 West University, Durant, OK 74730			(800) 522-6154
Ada	(405) 436-3190	Midwest City	(405) 733-7348
Alva	(405) 327-8608	Oklahoma City	(405) 232-1968
Durant	(405) 924-0277	Poteau	(918) 647-4019
Enid	(405) 242-7989	Tahlequah	(918) 458-0802
Langston	(405) 466-3256	Tulsa	(918) 583-2600

| Lawton | (405) 248-4946 | Weatherford | (405) 774-1040 |
| Miami | (918) 540-0575 | | |

Oklahoma Small Business Investment Companies
Oklahoma City-BancFirst Investment Corporation (405) 270-1000

Oklahoma Certified Development Companies
Burnes Flat-SWODA Development Corporation (405) 562-4882
Durant-Rural Enterprises, Inc. (405) 924-5094
Muskogee-Verd-Ark-Ca Developemtn Corporation (918) 683-4634
Oklahoma City-Metro Area Development Corporation (405) 424-5181
Tulsa-Small Business Capital Corporation (918) 599-6112
Tulsa-Tulsa Economic Development Corporation (918) 585-8332
Tulsa-Tulsa Economic Development (918) 585-8332

OREGON

Statewide Financing Information and Resources: **www.state.or.us**

Economic Development Office **(503) 986-0123**
775 Summer Street, NE, Salem, OR 97310

Economic Development
• Marketing Services (503) 986-0111
• Business Inforamation Center (503) 986-2222
  Business Start-ups Packets

Financial Assistance
• Business Finance Section (503) 986-0160

Minority/Women
• Oregon Department of Transportation (503) 986-2643
  Office of Minority, Women's & Emerging Small Businesses (503) 378-5651

Associated Oregon Industries, Inc. (503) 588-0050
1149 Court Street, NE, P.O. Box 12519, Salem, OR 97309

SBA District Office (503) 326-2682
222 South West Columbia St., Suite 500, Portland, OR 97201-6605

Oregon Small Business Development Centers
Lane Community College (541) 726-2250
44 West Broadway, Suite 501, Eugene, OR 97401-3021

Albany	(541) 917-4923	Milwaukie	(503) 656-4447
Ashland	(541) 772-3478	Ontario	(541) 889-2617
Bend	(541) 383-7290	Pendleton	(541) 276-6233
Coos Bay	(541) 888-7100	Portland	(503) 274-7482
Eugene	(541) 726-2255	Roseburg	(541) 672-2535
Grants Pass	(541) 471-3515	Salem	(503) 399-5088
Gresham	(503) 667-7658	Seaside	(503) 738-3347
Klamath Falls	(541) 885-1760	The Dalles	(541) 298-3118
LaGrande	(541) 962-3391	Tillamook	(503) 842-2551
Lincoln City	(541) 994-4166	Medford	(541) 772-3478

Oregon Small Business Investment Companies
Portland-Northern Pacifice Capital Corporation (503) 241-1255
Portland-Shaw Venture Partners III, LP (503) 228-4884

Oregon Certified Development Companies
Albany-Cascades West Financial Services, Inc. (541) 967-8551
Beaverton-Northwest Small Business Finance Corporation (503) 629-9662
Pendleton-Greater Eastern Oregon Development Corp. (541) 276-6745
Redmond-Oregon Certified Business Development Corp. (541) 672-6728

Micro Loans
Albany-Cascades West (541) 967-8551

PENNSYLVANIA

Statewide Financing Information and Resources: **www.state.pa.us**

Department of Commerce **(717) 783-8950**
400 Forum Building, Harrisburg, PA 17120

Economic Development
• Small Business Resource Center (717) 783-5700
• Office of Entrepreneurial Assistance (ARC Program) (717) 783-8950
• Office of Small Business Advocate (717) 783-2525

Financial Assistance
• Machine and Equipment Loan Fund (717) 783-5046
• Pennsylvania Capital Access Program (717) 783-1109
• Pennsylvania Capital Loan Fund (717) 783-1768
• Pennsylvania Economic Development Financing Authority (717) 783-1108
• Pennsylvania Industrial Development Authority (717) 787-6245

- Pennsylvania Minority Business Development Authority   (717) 783-1127
- Revenue Bond and Mortgage Program   (717) 783-1108

Minority/Women
- Women's Business Advocate and
  Entrepreneurial Assistance Office   (717) 787-3339
- Governor's Advisory Commission on
  African American Affairs   (717) 772-5085
- Governor's Advisory Commission on Latino Affairs   (717) 783-3877

Pennsylvania Chamber of Business & Industry   (717) 255-3252
One Commerce Square, 417 Walnut streeet, Harrisburg, PA 17101

SBA District Offices
Harrisburg (Branch Office)   (717) 782-3840
  100 Chrstnut Street, Room309, Harrisburg, PA 17101
King of Prussia   (610) 962-3800
  475 Allendale Road, Sute 201, King of Prusia, PA 19406
Pittsburgh   (412) 644-2780
  960 Penn Avenue, 5th Floor, Pittsburgh, PA 15222
Wiles-Barre (Branch Office)   (717) 826-6497
  20 N. Pennsylvania Ave, Room 2327, Wilkes-Barre, PA 18701-3589

Pennslyvania Small Business Development Centers
University of Pennsylvania, the Wharton School   (215) 898-1219
Vance Hall, 4th Floor, 3733 Spruce St., Philadelphia, PA 19104-6374

Bethlehem	(610) 758-3980	Loretto	(814) 472-3200
Clarion	(814) 226-2060	Philadelphia	(215) 204-7282
Erie	(814) 871-7714	Pittsburgh	(412) 396-6233
Harrisburgh	(717) 720-4230	Scanton	(717) 941-7588
Latrobe	(412) 537-4572	Wilkes-Barre	(717) 831-4340
Lewisburg	(717) 524-1249		

Pennsylvania Small Business Investment Companies
Malvern-CIP Capital, LP   (610) 695-2066
Philadelphia-Core State Enerprises   (215) 973-6519
Radnor-Meridian enture Partners   (610) 254-2999
Wayne-Grater Philadelphia Venture Capital Corp. Inc.   (610) 688-6829
Wayne-CIP Capital   (610) 964-7860

Pennsylvania Certified Development Companies
Allentown-Allentown Economic Development Corporation   (610) 435-8890
Altoona-Altoona-Blair County Development Corp.   (814) 944-6113

Butler-Community Development Corp. of Butler County	(412) 283-1961
Exton-South Eastern Econ. Development Co. of Pennsylvania	(610) 363-6110
Lewisburg-SEDA-COG Local Development Corporation	(717) 524-4491
Philadelphia-DelVal Business Fiance Corporation	(215) 871-3770
Philadelphia-PIDC Local Develoment Corporation	(215) 496-8020
Pittsburg-Pittsburg Countywide Corporation Inc.	(412) 471-1030

Micro Loans

Philadelphia-Ben Franklin Tech Center	(215) 382-0380
York-York County Industrial Dev.	(717) 846-8879

PUERTO RICO

Statewide Financing Information and Resources:	www.state.pr.us

Department of Economic Development & Commerce   **(787) 721-2898**
P.O. Box 4435, San Juan, PR 00902-4435

Economic Development
- Office of Ombudsman   (787) 724-7373
- Commercial Development Administration   (787) 721-3290

Financial Assistance
- Economic Development Bank for Puerto Rico   (787) 766-4300
- Economic Development Administration   (787) 758-4747
- Government Bank for Puerto Rico   (787) 722-3760

Chamber of Commerce of Puerto Rico   (787) 721-3290
100 Tetuan Street, Old San Juan, PR 00901

SBA District Office   (787) 766-5572
Citibank Bldg, 252 Ponce de Leon Ave., Sutie 201, Hato Rey, PR 00918

Puerto Rico Small Business Development Centers
Edifico Union Plaza (787) 763-6811
Suite 701, 416 Ponca De Leon Ave., hato Rey, PR 00918

Humacao	(809) 850-2500	Ponce	(809) 841-2641
San Juan	(809) 765-2335	Rio Piedras	(809) 763-5880

Pureto Rico Small Business Investment Company

Hato Rey-North America Investment Corporation	(787) 754-6178

Puerto Rico Certified Development Companies

Hato Rey- Corp. para el Fomento Econ. de la Ciudad Capital (787) 756-5080
Hato Rey-North Puerto Rico Local Developemnt Co., Inc.   (787) 754-7474
Orocvis-Caciques Development Corporations   (787) 876-2520
San Juan-La Marketing Development Corporation   (787) 765-0801
Santurce-Advancer Local Developoment Corporation   (787) 721-6797

Micro Loans

Rio Piedras-Corp. for the Economic Devleopment
    of the City of San Juan   (787) 756-5080

RHODE ISLAND

Statewide Financing Information and Resources:	**www.state.ri.us**

Rhode Island Economic Development Corporation	**(401) 277-2601**
1 West Exchange Street, Providence, RI 02903	

Economic Development
*   Business Development Division   (401) 277-2601

Financial Assistance
*   Financing Programs   (401) 277-2601
*   Small Business Loan Fund   (401) 277-2601

Greater Providence Chamber of Commerce	(401) 521-5000
30 Exchange Terrace, Providence, RI 02903	

SBA District Office	(401) 528-4584
380 Westminister Street, Providence, RI 02903	

Rhode Island Small Business Development Centers
Bryant College SBDC   (401) 232-6111
1150 Douglas Pike, Smithfield, RI 02917-1282
Lincoln   (401) 334-1000   Middletown   (401) 849-6900
North Kingstown (401) 294-1228   Newport   (401) 849-6900
Providence   (401) 831-1330

Rhode Island Small Business Investment Companies
Cranston-Domestic Capital Corporation   (401) 946-3310
Providence-Fleet Equity Partners VI, LP   (401) 278-6770
Providence-Fllet Venture Resources, Inc.   (401) 278-6770
Providence-Moneta Capital Corporation   (401) 454-7500

Rhode Island Certified Development Company
Providence-Ocean State Business Development Authority   (401) 454-4560

Micro Loans
None

SOUTH CAROLINA

Statewide Financing and Information Resources:	**www.state.sc.us**

Governor's Office-Small and Minority Business Assistance   **(803) 734-0657**
1205 Pendleton Street, Columbia , SC 29201

Economic Development
• Existing Business and Industry Services Department   (803) 737-0400

Financial Assistance
• Jobs Economic Develpment Authority   (803) 737-0079

Minority/Women
• Office of Small and Minority Business Assistance   (803) 734-0657

South Carolina Chamber of Commerce   (803) 799-4601
1201 Main Street, Suite 1810, Columbia, SC 29201

SBA District Office   (803) 765-5377
1835 Assembly Street, Room 358, Columbia, SC 29201

South Carolina Small Business Development Centers
University of South Carolina   (803) 777-4907
College of Business Administration, Columbia, SC 29208

Aiken	(803) 64103646	Florence	(803) 661-8256
Beaufort	(803) 521-4143	Greenville	(864) 250-8894
Charleston	(803) 740-6160	Greenwood	(803) 941-8071
Clemson	(803) 656-3227	Orangeburg	(803) 536-8445
Columbia	(803) 777-5118	Rock Hill	(803) 323-2283
Conway	(803) 349-2170	Spartanburg	(864) 594-5080

South Carolina Small Business Investment Companies
Charleston-Charleston Capital Corporation   (803) 723-6464
Greenville-Reedy River Ventures   (864) 232-6198

South Carolina Certified Development Companies

Columbia-Certified Development Corp. of South Carolina	(803) 798-4064
Rock Hill-Catawaba Regional Dev.	(803) 327-9041
Spartanburg-Cit of Spartanburg Development Corporation	(864) 596-2108
Sumter-Santee-Lynches Regional Development Corporation	(803) 775-7381

Micro Loans

Charlesto-Charlesto Citywide Local Dev. Corp.	(803) 724-3796

SOUTH DAKOTA

Statewide Financing Information and Resources:	**www.state.sd.us**

Governor's Office of Economic Development   **(605) 773-5032**
711 East Wells Avenue, Pierre, SD 57501-3369

Economic Development
- Economic Locaiton Services   (605) 773-5032
- Business Research Bureau   (605) 677-5287

Financial Assistance
- Financial Packaging   (605) 773-5032
- Economic Development Finance Authority   (605) 773-5032
- Revolving Economic Development and Initiative Fund   (605) 773-5032

Industry & Commerce Association of South Dakota   (605) 224-6161
108 North Euclid Avenue, P.O. Box 190, Pierre, SD 57501

SBA District Office   (605) 330-4231
110 South Phillips, Suite 200, Sioux Falls, SD 57102-1109

South Dakota Small Business Development Centers
University of South Dakota   (605) 677-5498
School of Business
Patterson Hall 115, 414 EAst Clarke Street, Vermillion, SD 57069

Aberdeen	(605) 626-2565	Sioux Falls	(605) 367-5753
Rapid City	(605) 394-5311		

South Dakota Certified Development Companies

Pierre-South Dakota Development Corporation	(605) 773-5032
Speanfish-Northern Hills Community Dev.	(605) 642-7106
Watertown-First District Development Company	(605) 886-7225

Micro Loans
Kyle-Lakota Fund   (605) 455-2500

TENNESSEE

Statewide Financing Information and Resource: **www.state.tn.us**

Department of Econmic and Community Development   **(800) 872-7201**
320 Sixth Avenue North, Nashville, TN 37243

Economic Development
- Small Business Office   (615) 741-2626
- Center for Industrial Services   (615) 532-8657
- SCORE   (615) 736-7621

Minority/Women
- Office of Minority Business Enterprise   (615) 741-2545
- Women Business Owners   (615) 741-2545
- Minority Business Deveelopment Center   (615) 255-0432

Tennessee Assocaition of Business   (615) 256-5141
611 Commerce Street, Suite 3030, Nashville, TN 37203-3742

SBA District Office   (615) 736-5881
50 Advantage Way, Suite 201, Nashville, TN 37228-1500

Tennessee Small Business Development Centers
Unviersity of Memphis   (901) 678-2500
South Campus (Getwell Road), Building #1, Memphis, TN 38152

Chattanooga	(423) 266-5781	Johnson City	(423) 439-5630
Chattanooga	(423) 752-1774	Kingsport	(423) 392-8017
Clarksville	(615) 648-7764	Knoxville	(423) 525-0277
Cleveland	(423) 478-6247	Memphis	(901) 527-1041
Columbia	(615) 898-2745	Morristown	(423) 585-2675
Dyersburg	(901) 286-3201	Murfreesboro	(615) 898-2745
Hartsville	(615) 374-9521	Nashville	(615) 963-7179
Jackson	(901) 424-5389		

Tennessee Small business Investment Companies
Chattanooga-Valley Capital Corporation   (423) 265-1557
Memphis-West Tennessee Venture Capital Corporation   (901) 522-9237
Nashville-Equitas   (615) 383-8673

Nashville-Pacific Capital, LP (615) 292-3166
Nashville-Sirrom Capital Corporation (615) 256-0701

Tennessee Certified Development Companies
Chattanooga-Southeast Local Development Corporation (423) 266-5781
Columbia-Sout Central Tennessee Business
    Development Corp. (615) 381-2041
Knoxville-Areawide Development Corporation (423) 588-7972
Nashville-Mid-Cumberland Area Development Corporation (615) 862-8831

TEXAS

Statewide Financing Information and Resources: **www.state.tx.us**

Texas Department of Commerce **(512) 936-0100**
1700 North Congress Avenue, P.O. Box 12728, Austin, TX 78711

Economic Development
- Texas One (512) 936-0237
- Business Development Division (512) 936-0223
- Information and Research (512) 936-0081
- Business Information and Referral (800) 888-0581
- Growth-Retention (512) 936-0254
- Community Assistance/Small Business (512) 936-0223

Financial Assistance
- Business Services (512) 936-0282
- Capital Development (512) 936-0260
- Enterprise Zone (512) 936-0270
- Smart Jobs (512) 936-0500
- Texas Manufacturing Assistance Center (512) 936-0235

Minority/Women
- Community assistance/Small Business (512) 936-0223

Other Key Texas Phone Numbers

Texas Association of Business and Chambers of Commerce (512) 472-1594
1209 Nueces, Austin, TX 78701

SBA District Offices
Corpus Christi (Branch Office) (512) 888-3331
    606 N. Carancahua, Suite 1200, Corpus Christi, TX 78476

El Paso   (915) 540-5155
    10737 Gateway West, Suite 114, Ft. Worth, TX 76155
Harlingen   (210) 427-8625
    222 E. Van Buren Street, Room 500, Harlingen, TX 78550-6855
Houston   (713) 773-6500
    9301 Southwest Freeway, Suite 550, Houston, TX 77074-1591
Lubbock   (806) 743-7462
    1611 Tenth Street, Suite 200, lubbock, TX 79401-2693
San Antonio   (210) 472-5900
    727 E. Durango Blve. Suite A-527, San Antonio, TX 78206-1204

Texas Small Business Develoment Centers
Dallas County Community College, North Texas SBDC   (214) 565-5831
    1402 Corinth Street, Suite3 2111, Dallas, TX 75215
Houston Small Business Development Center   (713) 752-8400
    1100 Louisiana, Suite 500, Houston, TX 77002
Lubbock Small Business Development Center   (806) 745-3973
    2579 South Loop 289, Lubbock, TX 79423
University of Texas, San Antionio   (210) 558-2460
    1222 North Main, San Antonio, TX 78212

Abilene	(915) 670-0300	Alpine	(915) 837-8694
Alvin	(713) 388-4686	Huntsville	(409) 294-3737
Amarillo	(806) 372-5151	Kingsville	(512) 595-5088
Athens	(903) 675-7403	Lake Jackson	(409) 266-3380
Austin	(512) 473-3510	Laredo	(210) 722-0563
Baytown	(713) 425-6309	Longview	(903) 757-5857
Beaumont	(409) 880-2367	Lubbock	(806) 745-1637
Bonham	(903) 583-4811	Brenham	(409) 830-4137
Lufkin	(409) 639-1887	Bryan	(409) 260-5222
Mt. Pleasant	(800) 357-7232	Corpus Christi	(512) 881-1888
Odessa	(915) 552-2455	Corsicana	(903) 874-0658
Paris	(903) 784-1802	Dallas	(214) 565-5842
Plano	(214) 985-3770	San Angelo	(915) 942-2098
San Antonio	(210) 558-2458	Stafford	(713) 933-7932
Dension	(903) 786-3551	Stephenville	(817) 968-9330
Houston-Charter Venture			(713) 692-6121
Duncanville	(214) 709-5878	Edinburg	(210) 316-2610
Tyler	(903) 510-2975	El Paso	(915) 534-3410
Uvalde	(210) 278-2527	Fort Worth	(817) 794-5978
Victoria	(512) 575-8944	Gainesville	(817) 668-4220
Waco	(817) 750-3600	Galveston	(409) 740-7380
Wichita Falls	(817) 689-4373	Grand Prairie	(214) 565-5850
Houston	(713) 591-9320		

Texas Small Business Investment Companies

Dallas-alliance Enterprise Corporation	(972) 991-1597
Dallas-AMT Capital	(214) 905-9760
Dallas-Banc One Capital Partners Corpoation	(214) 979-4360
Dallas-Capotal Southwest Venture Corporaation	(214) 233-8242
Dallas-Mapleleaf Capital, Ltd.	(214) 239-5650
Dallas-NationsBanc Capital Corporation	(214) 508-0900
Dallas-North Texas MESBIC, Inc.	(214) 991-8060
Dallas-PMC Investment Corporation	(214) 380-0044
Dallas-Stratford Capital Parnters, LP	(214) 740-7377
Dallas-Western Financial Capital Corporation	(214) 380-0044
Fort Worth-HCT Capital Corporation	(817) 763-8706
Fort Worth-SBIC Partners, LP	(817) 339-7020
Houston-Alliance Business Investment Co.	(713) 659-3131
Houston-The Catalyst Fund, Inc.	(713) 623-8133
Houston-Charter Venture	(713) 692-6121
Houston-Chen's Financial Group, Inc.	(713) 772-8868
Houston-Houston Partners, SBIP	(713) 222-8600
Houston-MSBIC Financial Corporation of Houston	(713) 869-4061
Houston-SBI Capital Corporation	(713) 975-1188
Houston-UNCO Ventures, Ltd.	(713) 622-9595
Houston-Ventex Partners, Ltd.	(713) 659-7860
San Antonio-First Capital Group	(210) 736-4233

Texas Certified Development Companies

Abilene-Council Finance	(915) 672-8544
Amarillo-Texas Panhandle Regional Development Corp.	(806) 372-3381
Austin-Capital Certified Development Corporation	(512) 936-0223
Austin-Cen-Tex Certified Development Corporation	(512) 473-3500
Austin-Texas Certified Development Company	(512) 476-8939
Beaumont-Southeast Texas Economic Devel. Foundation	(409) 838-6581
Brownsville-Brownsville Local Development Company Inc.	(210) 548-6150
Bryan-Bryan College Station Certified Development Co.	(409) 775-3699
Dallas-Dallas Business Finance	(214) 428-7332
El Paso-Upper Rio Grande Development Company	(915) 533-0998
Fort Worth-Fort Worth Economic Development Corporation	(817) 336-6420
Houston-Houston-Galveston Area Local Development Corp.	(713) 627-3200
Kilgore-East Texas Regional Development Company, Inc.	(903) 984-3989
Lubbock-Caprock Business Finance Corporation, Inc.	(806) 762-8721
McAllen-Lower Rio Grande Valley Certified Devel. Corp.	(210) 682-3481
Plano-North Texas Certified Development Corporation	(241) 516-0514
San Antonio-San Antonio Local Development Corporation	(210) 207-3932
Texarkana-Ark-Tex Regional Development Company, Inc.	(903) 798-3955
Waco-Central Texas Certified Development Company	(871) 799-0259

Micro Loans
Dallas-Southern Dallas Development Corp. (214) 428-7332

UTAH

Statwide Financing Information and Resources: www.state.ut.us

Community and Economic Development **(801) 538-8700**
324 South State Street, Sutie 500, Salt Lake City, UT 84111

Economic Development
- Business Expansion & Retention (801) 538-8775
- Small Business Development Center (801) 255-5991

Financial Assistance
- Economic Development Corporation of Utah (801) 538-8775
- Utah Capital Access Act (801) 538-8776
- Utah Microenterprise Loan Fund (801) 269-8408
- Utah Technology Finance Corporation (801) 364-4346

Minority Opportunities
- Office of Black Affairs (801) 538-8829
- Office of Hispanic Affairs (801) 538-8850
- Office of Indian Affairs (801) 538-8808

Utah State Chamber of Commerce Association (801) 467-0844
c/o Sugar House Area Chamber of Commerce
1095 East 2100 South, Salt Lake City, UT 8413

SBA District Office (801) 524-3209
125 South State St., Room 2237, Salt Lake City, UT 84138-1195

Utah Small Business Development Centers
Salt Lake Community College (801) 957-3480
1623 State St., Salt Lake City, UT 84115

Cedar City	(801) 586-5400	Orem	(801) 222-8230
Ephraim	(801) 283-4021	Price	(801) 637-5032
Logan	(801) 797-2277	Roosevelt	(801) 722-4523
Ogden	(801) 626-7232	St. George	(801) 652-7732
Moab	(801) 626-6070		

Utah Small Business Investment Companies
Salt Lake City-First Security Business Investment Corp.   (801) 246-5737
Salt Lake City-Wasatch Venture   (801) 524-8939

Utah Certified Development Company
Midvale-Deseret Certified Development Company   (801) 566-1163
Ogden-Northern Utah Capital   (801) 627-1333

Micro Loans
Salt Lake City-Utah Tech, Finance   (801) 364-4346

VERMONT

Statwide Financing Information and Resources: **www.state.vt.us**

Vermont Department of Economic Development   **(802) 828-3221**
109 State Street, Montpelier, VT 05602

Economic Development
• Small Business Development Center   (802) 728-9101

Financial Assistance
• Vermont Economic Development Authority   (802) 223-7226

Minority/Women
• Government Assistance Prgram   (802) 828-3221

Vermont Chamber of Commerce   (802) 223-3443
P.O. Box 37, Montpelier, VT 05601

SBA District Office   (802) 828-4422
87 State Street, Room 205, P.O. box 605, Montpelier, VT 05601

Vermont Small Business Development Centers
Vermont Technical College   (802) 728-9101
P.O. Box 422, Randolph, VT0 5060-0422   (800) 464-SBDC
Brattleboro   (802) 258-3886   North Bennington   (802) 422-8975
Burlington   (802) 658-9228   Rutland   (802) 773-9147
Middlebury   (802) 388-7953   Springfield   (802) 885-2071
Montpelier (EDC) (802) 223-4654
St. Johnsbury   (802) 748-1014

Vermont Small Business Investment Company
Waterbury-Green Mountain Capital, LP   (802) 244-8981

Vermont Certified Development Companies
Montpelier-Central Vermont Economic Development Corp.   (802) 223-4654
Montpelier-Vermont 503 Corporation   (802) 828-5627
St. Johnsbury-Northern Community Investment Corp.   (802) 748-5101

Micro-Loans
St. Albams-economic Development Council
   of Northern Vermont   (802) 524-4546

VIRGINIA

Statewide Financing Information and Resources: **www.stae.va.us**

Virginia Small Business Development Network
Virginia Department of Economic Development   **(804) 371-8253**
P.O. Box 798, Richmond, VA 23206-0798

Economic Development
• Small Business Development Center   (804) 371-8253

Financial Assistance
• Virginia Small Business Financing Authority   (804) 371-8254

Minority/Womens
• Department of Minority Business Enterprise   (804) 786-5560

The Virginia Chamber of Commerce   (804) 644-1607
9 South Fifth Street, Richmond, VA 23219

SBA District Office   (804) 771-2400
1504 Santa Rosa Road, Suite 200, Richmond, VA 23229

Virginia Small Business Development Centers
Commonwealth of Virginia Dept. of Economic Devel.   (804) 371-8253
Virginia Business Development Network
901 East Byrd Street, West Tower, 19th Floor, Richmond, VA 23206

Abingdon	(540) 676-5615	Lynchburg	(804) 582-6170
Alexandria	(703) 299-9146	Manassas	(703) 335-2500
Arlington	(703) 993-8182	Middletown	(540) 869-6649
Belle Haven	(757) 442-7179	Richlands	(540) 964-7345

Charlottesville	(804) 295-8198	Richmond	(800) 646-7232
Fairfax	(703) 277-7700	Roanoke	(540) 983-0717
Farmville	(804) 395-2086	South Boston	(804) 575-0044
Fredericksburg	(540) 654-1060	Sterling	(703) 430-7222
Hampton	(757) 825-295	Warsaw	(804) 333-0286
Harrisonburg	(540) 568-3227	Wytheville	(540) 223-4798

Virginia Small Business Investment Companies

Arlington-Continental SBIC	(703) 527-5200
McLean-East West United Investment Company	(703) 442-0150
Virginia Beach-Eastern Virginia SBIC	(757) 626-1111
Vienna-Walnut Capital Corporation	(703) 448-3771

Virginia Certified Development Companies

Charlottesville-Virginia Economic Development Corporation	(804) 979-0114
Fredericksburg-Rappahannock Economic Development Corp.	(800) 627-2892
Norfolk-Urban Business Development Corporation	(757) 623-2691
Petersburg-Crater Development Company	(804) 861-1666
Portsmouth-Portsmouth Certified Development Corporation	(757) 393-8989
Richmond-James River Certified Development Corporation	(804) 788-6966
South Hill-Lake Country Development Corporation	(804) 447-7101
Sterling-Virginia Asset Financing	(703) 421-0504

Micro Loans

Arlington-Ethiopian Community Development	(703) 685—510
Lynchburg-Business Development Center	(804) 582-6100

WASHINGTON

Statewide Financing Information and Resources: www.state.wa.us

Business Assistance Center
Department of Community, Trade and Economic Development **(360) 753-4900**
906 Columbia Street SW, P.O. Box 48300, Olympia, WA 98504-8300

Economic Development
- Business Assistance Hotline   (800) 237-1233
- Business Development   (206) 464-7255
- Innovation and tech. Development Assistance Program   (206) 464-5450
- Small Business Development Center   (509) 335-1576
- Small Business Ombudsman   (360) 586-3022
- Small Business Hotline   (360) 664-9501

Financial Assistance
- Community Development Finance Program   (360) 753-4900
- Development Loan Fund   (360) 753-4900
- Small Business Finance Unit   (360) 753-4900
- Washington Economic Development Finance Authority   (206) 389-2559

Minority/Women
- Minority and Women's Business Development   (206) 389-2561

Association of Washington Business   (360) 943-1600
P.O. Box 658, 1414 South Cherry St., OLympia, WA 98507-0658

SBA District Offices
Seattle   (206) 553-7310
    1200 Sixth Avenue, Suite 1700, Seattle, WA 98101-1128
Spokane   (509) 353-2810
    West 601 First Avenue, Tenth Floor, Spokane, WA 99204-0317

Washington Small Business Development Centers
Washington State University   (509) 335-1576
Johnson Tower 501, Pullman, WA 99164-4851

Aberdeen	(360) 538-4021	Seattle	(206) 553-5615
Bellevue	(206) 643-2888	Spokane	(509) 358-7544
Bellingham	(360) 676-2170	Tacoma	(206) 272-7232
Centralia	(360) 736-9391	Vancouver	(360) 260-6372
Kennewick	(509) 735-6222	Walla Walla	(509) 527-4681
Lynwood	(206) 640-1435	Wenatchee	(509) 662-8016
Moses Lake	(509) 762-6289	Yakima	(509) 574-4940
Mt. Vernon	(360) 416-7872	Okanagan	(509) 826-5107
Olympia	(360) 753-5616	Port Angeles	(360) 457-7793

Washington Small Business Investment Companies
Bellevue-Pacific Northwest Partners   (206) 646-7357

Washington Certified Development Companies
Dennewick-Southeastern Washington Development Assoc.   (509) 735-1000
Seattle-Evergreen Community Development Association   (206) 622-3731
Spokane-Greater Spokane Business Devleopment Association (509) 458-8555

Micro Lenders
Everett-Snohomish County Private Industry   (206) 743-9669

WEST VIRGINIA

Statewide Financing Information and Resources: www.state.wv.us

Development Office   **(304) 558-2234**
Department of Commerce
Capitol Complex, Bldg. 6, room 525, Charleston, WV 25305

Economic Development
- Small Business Development Center   (304) 558-3650

Financial Assistance
- West Virginia Economic Development Authority   (304) 558-3650

West Virginia Chamber of Commerce   (304) 342-1115
1314 Virginia Street East, P.O. Box 2789, Charleston, WV 25330-2789

SBA District Offices
Charleston (Branch Office)   (304) 347-5220
    550 Eagan Street, Room 309, Charleston, WV 25301
Clarksburg   (304) 623-5631
    168 West Main Street, Sixth Floor, Clarksburg, WV 26301

West Virginia Small Business Development Center
West Virginia Development Office   (304) 558-2960
950 Kanawha Blvd. East, Charleston, WV 25301

Beckley	(304)255-4022	Morgantown	(304) 293-5839
Fairmont	(304) 367-4125	Parkersburg	(304) 424-8277
Huntington	(304) 696-6789	Shepherdstown	(304) 876-5261
Montgomery	(304) 422-5501	Wheeling	(304) 233-5900 x4206

West Virginia Certified Development Companies
Charleston-West Virginia Certified Development Corp.   (304) 558-3691
Oak Hill-4-C Certified Development Corporation   (304) 469-3972
Wheeling-OVIBDC CDC, Inc.   (304) 232-7722

WISCONSIN

Statewide Financing Information and Resources: www.state.wi.us

Department of Development   **(608) 266-1018**
123 West Washington Avenue, P.O. Box 7970, Madison, WI 53707

Economic Development
- Bureau of Business Development   (608) 266-1386
- Bureau of Business & Industry Services   (608) 267-0313
- Small Business Ombudsman   (608) 267-9384

Financial Assistance
- Wisconsin Business Development Finance Corporation   (608) 258-8830
- Wisconsin Development Fund   (608) 266-1018
- Wisconsin Housing and Economic Development Authority (800) 334-6873

Minority/Women
- Bureau of Minority Business Development   (608) 267-9550
- Women's Business Liaison   (608) 266-9944
- Wisconsin Housing and Economic Development Authority (800) 334-6873

Wisconsin Manufacturers and Commerce   (608) 258-3400
501 E. Washington Avenue, P.O. Box 352, Madison, WI 53701-0352

SBA District
Madison   (608) 264-5261
    212 East Washington Avenue, Room 213, Madison, WI 53703
Milwaukee (Branch Office)   (414) 297-3941
    310 West Wisconsin Avenue, Suite 400, Milwaukee, WI 53203

Wisconsin Small Business Development Centers
University of Wisconsin   (608) 263-7794
432 North Lake Street, Room 423, Madison, WI 53706

Eau Claire	(715) 836-5811	Milwaukee	(414) 227-3240
Green Bay	(414) 465-2089	Oshkosh	(414) 424-1453
Kenosha	(414) 595-2189	Stevens Point	(715) 346-2004
La Crosse	(608) 785-8782	Superior	(715) 394-8351
Madison	(608) 263-2221	Whitewater	(414) 472-3217

Wisconsin Small Business Investment Companies
Brookfield-Bando-McGlocklin SBIC   (414) 784-9010
Brokfield-Polaris Capital Corporation   (414) 637-8388 x127
Milwaukee-Banc One Venture Corporation   (414) 765-2274
Milwaukee-Future Value Ventures, Inc.   (414) 278-0377
Milwaukee-InvestAmerica Investment Advisors, Inc.   (414) 276-3839
Milwaukee-M & I Ventures Corporation   (414) 765-7910
Milwaukee-MorAmerica Capital Corporation   (414) 276-3839

Wisconsin Certified Development Companies

Almera-Western Wisconsin Development Corporations	(715) 357-6282
Eau-Claire-Wisconsin Business Development Finance Corp.	(715) 834-9474
Green Bay-Great Lakes Asset Corproation	(414) 499-6444
Kenosha-Kenosha Area Development Corporation	(414) 605-1101
Madison-Madison Development Corporation	(608) 256-2799
Madison-Wisconsin Business Development Finance Corp.	(608) 258-8830
Milwaukee-Milwaukee Economic Development Corporation	(414) 286-5840
Racine-Racine County Business Development Corporation	(414) 638-0234
Waukesha-Waukesha County Associate Development Corp.	(414) 695-7900

WYOMING

Statewide Financing Information and Resources: **www.state.wy.us**

Division of Economic and Community Development   **(307) 777-7284**
6101 Yellowstone Road, Fourth Floor, Cheyenne, WY 82002

Economic Development
- DECD Business Development Section   (307) 777-7284
- Business/Enterpreneur Assistance   (307) 777-7133

Financial Assistance
- Wyomic Industrial Development Corporation (WIDC)   (307) 234-5351
- DECD Small Grants Program   (307) 777-7284

Wyoming Department of Transportation   (307) 777-4457
   -Disadvantaged Business Assistance

Wyoming Department of Employment   (307) 777-7672

SBA District Office   (307) 261-6500
100 East B Street, Federal Bldg., Room 4001, P.O. Box 2839,
Casper, WY 82602-2839

Wyoming Small Business Development Centers

University of Wyoming			(307) 766-3505
P.O. Box 3622, Laramie, WY 82071-3622			(800) 348-5194
Casper	(307) 234-6683	Powell	(307) 754-2139
Cheyenne	(307) 632-6141	Rock Springs	(307) 352-6894

Micro Loans
None

BIBLIOGRAPHY

Bel Air, Roger. *How to Borrow Money From A Banker.* New York: AMACOM, 1988.

DeThomas, Art. *Financing Your Small Business.* Oasis Press, 1992.

Langstaff, Margot: *The Colorado Guide To Financing Sources.* Financial Education Publishers, 1995.

Nicholas, Ted. *43 Proven Ways To Raise Capital For Your Small Business.* Enterprise Printing, 1991.

SBA Office of Advocacy. *Small Business Assistance.* U.S. Government Printing Office, 1997.

INDEX

OTHER PEOPLE'S MONEY

Cover design by Eric Norton

*Text design by Mary Jo Zazueta in New
Baskerville and Myriad Roman*

Text stock is 60 lb. Offset White

Printed and bound by Data Reproductions

Client Liaison: Theresa Nelson

Production Editor: Alex Moore